The Healing Gifts
of the Spirit

The Healing Gifts of the Spirit

By Agnes Sanford

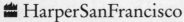 HarperSanFrancisco
A Division of HarperCollins*Publishers*

A hardcover edition of this work was published by J. B. Lippincott Company.

THE HEALING GIFTS OF THE SPIRIT. Copyright © 1966 by Agnes Sanford. All rights reserved. Printed in the United States of America. No part of this book may be used or reproduced in any manner whatsoever without written permission except in the case of brief quotations embodied in critical articles and reviews. For information address HarperCollins Publishers, 10 East 53rd Street, New York, NY 10022.

FIRST HARPER & ROW PAPERBACK EDITION PUBLISHED IN 1984.

Library of Congress Cataloging in Publication Data

Sanford, Agnes Mary White.
    THE HEALING GIFTS OF THE SPIRIT.

    1. Spiritual healing.   2. Gifts, Spiritual.   I. Title.
[BT732.5.S233   1984]   234'.13   83-48998
ISBN 0-06-067052-5 (pbk.)

To John Loren Sandford

Contents

Introduction

WE LIVE PRECARIOUSLY IN TWO WORLDS, BOTH IN TIME and beyond time, both in space and beyond space. Some of us think naïvely that we know ourselves: the I, the ego, the self, the being who is visible, who speaks in an audible tone, who thinks in words that the mind can hear. But what of the rest of the I: the long train that follows the I and attaches itself, as the tail of a comet follows its bright center in and out of the years and of the aeons? Who and what is this other part and when and where has it lived or will it live? Can it by any chance remember the dark sea where countless ages ago its dim life may have begun through light shining into darkness: the rays of the sun bent into the ever-shifting blues of the ocean until the life-giver and the life-receiver brought forth life? Can this be the reason why a visit to the seashore on a day of cold fog when one could hear only the breakers crashing beneath the boardwalk of the Jersey coast— why even this brief non-seeing glimpse of that old mother of life brought tears to my eyes, tears that fell for no reason that the conscious mind could know, but that touched an inner spring—that opened an inner door. . . . What spring? What door?

Reincarnation, some of you are no doubt thinking wisely. No. It is not so simple as that, this all-embracing mystery. Nor will the mere saying of a word bring wisdom, for words sometimes limit our knowledge, labeling a thing too glibly, so that we may go our way in specious content thinking that we know when we do not know.

Do I then know? Can I explain this matter of the involvement of many beings within us: those on whom we may place the finger and say "This is I," those who are not at all ourselves, those who lift up our hearts and those who cast them down? No, I do not know. But this much I do know: that this unseen part of me, whether submerged beneath the depths of my conscious self or rising above it, whether descending into hell or ascending into heaven, this also is myself. And if I am to be a whole person, this area of emanation and of interpenetration must also be healed. I call this part of me the soul, or the "psyche." I might instead say "the unconscious" or "the subconscious," or "the deep mind" or the "spirit."

And although I do not understand all wisdom and all knowledge, I have found certain simple and practical ways of healing the soul, or the subconscious, as well as healing the body. In fact, of recent years my interest has veered away from the healing of the body and has been guided almost entirely into this deeper area: the healing of the "soul." For, unless the soul is healed, of what use is the wholeness of the body? Out of the depths come sudden changes of being which are more subtle than the changes in the air when the barometer is falling, and less explainable. As I look up from the typewriter, for instance, I see a lake, mist-bound, deep and silver under a dim sky. On its surface, gently shimmering even through the darkness, wild ducks wheel and dive and swim, weaving intricate patterns of beauty. Others float motionless, living creatures resting upon the mother of life, deeply content within themselves. Douglas firs rise tall and dark beyond the lake, enclosing in a stately frame the little world of water and of birds. In the far distance stands Mount Rainier. Beyond this magic and mysterious mountain that the Indians call "Home of the Gods" there rests eternally the blue sky, equally magic and mysterious. But today one cannot see mountain or sky, any more than one can see the waves of sight and of sound and of energy and of thought that fill the circumambient air, for the mist enfolds the world in a gentle hush and creates a different kind of beauty. I behold that beauty and my heart is stilled and my mind is rested. But on another morning I have sat by this same window and have been totally unable to enter into beauty; thinking only with impatience, "When will the clouds break? When will I see Mount Rainier, dressed in shining snow and lifting her tall head like the queen of all the thunders? When will the lake shine turquoise and lapis lazuli beneath the overhanging firs? When will the birds arise and cut the sky with sharp and silver wings instead of moping on that dark lake like dead things?"

What is it? Who is dead? The birds or I myself?

Yes, it is I who am like a dead thing. Not the birds. But what can I do about it? For I do not know what is wrong within me! In fact, on the worst days of all I do not even know anything is wrong, but accept this apathetic creature as myself. *Myself!* Have I forgotten the time when my feet had wings and my eyes saw beauty in every clod and stone and every dying leaf and every wisp of wind-blown cloud? Have I swallowed and digested the unpalatable thought that such an one was but the child I used to be and this now—this heavy-footed female grimly doing her duty —this is myself? If so I have buried myself already and need not wait for the funeral service, for life has said it over me.

What, then, can I do on these worst days of all—or better yet, what can someone else do for me? My work has been in helping others, and I am far more proficient at that than in helping myself. My own method is not so much to try to lift myself by my own bootstraps, which to my impatient nature is far too tedious, but to seek a helper. This may be one who understands and can guide my thinking, or it may be merely a friend who, while not understanding, can nevertheless pray for me.

Both methods of help are good. In fact I am coming to believe that both are necessary for the complete healing of the soul—insofar as any healing can be complete in this world which is such a small segment of real life.

From the very beginning religion has been a subjective experience rather than an organized system. The Bible has far more to say about the depths of personality and the power of God as able to operate therein, even to a point that Jesus calls rebirth, than it does about preachers and programs, campaigns and committees, budgets and canvasses, and hymnbooks and prayerbooks. In fact, the debasing of Christianity into something materialistic and, as we are pleased to call it, "rationalistic" is one of the tragedies of our modern life.

"But surely," some of you are thinking, "if we ask Jesus to save our souls He will do so!" Yes, He will. But not always without understanding, not always without a struggle toward God, not always without a learning of the power and a receiving of those gifts of the Spirit which are the spiritual tool kit with which we may do the works of Our Lord. One great trouble with the static system of righteous living that we are pleased to call Christianity today is that we are deceived by words. "I am saved," we say when we have had one experience of the love of Christ. But the experience dims, the love fades away, out of the deep mind there arise miasmas of darkness that choke our thinking and bind our souls in chains and we still say, "I am saved." Often with a deep inner sadness—for was this all that it meant: the shining and the glory, the melting warmth of love?

In one sense probably we are saved. Having once given ourselves to the Lord I believe that He will watch over us and will by some means or other shepherd us into heaven. But in another sense we most certainly are not saved! We are not saved from the darkness of despair nor from the sterility of frustration nor from the freezing effects of lovelessness nor from the weight of a benumbing sadness. And being unsaved from these burdens of life it is not too likely that we shall be able to show forth the love and joy of Christ to the world and thus save others.

Nowadays there is a great awakening from this state of torpor, a tremendous urge toward the real power of the indwelling spirit of God who is indeed able to transform us into new creatures in Christ Jesus. All over the world there are people rushing forth to lay hands on eager seekers and to pray that they receive the Baptism of the Spirit. This can be good, but it is strong medicine, and strong medicine should not be given without a knowledge and understanding of the particular weaknesses and tendencies of the one to whom it is given.

This I am in a position to know, having had many people come to me in trouble because they had been urged or even pushed into a spiritual experience when the soul was not ready to receive it. Some were in deep trouble because the spiritual experience in the higher areas of the unconscious—what one might call one's spirit—had increased the strain between an already unsteady ego and those mysterious forces that activate it from the depths, and this other even more mysterious energy imposed upon it from the heights. In a lesser trouble others found themselves not mentally depressed or disturbed, but apathetic: "I do not feel the joy," they tell me, and my heart yearns over them for they have been burnt over by a power that did not sink into the unhealed soul. And being burnt over did not make it easier to accept the real power and the real joy of this third Person of the Trinity: this third manifestation of the one ever-living Spirit who is God.

To the Mental Depressive

I WAS HEALED, FIRST OF ALL, OF MENTAL DEPRESSION. Do you know what mental depression is? Let me describe some of its symptoms, that you may read them and rejoice. For they were healed, every one, so that to remember them is a delight. When I wake in the morning nowadays, and my mind turns to the day's plan, I recall the days when I dragged myself out of bed and thought, "Another day; well, I have got through a lot of them and I'll probably get through this one too," and I laugh. As I glory in the sunshine, seeing how it lights blue flames upon tree leaves and how it sows the lake with diamonds, I recall the days when sunlight lay upon my soul as heavily as blackness and I thank the Lord that those old days are gone. As I remember the cold fear that at one time would hold me in an agonizing grip if husband or child did not come home on time, I am amazed that nowadays I cannot recall the actual feelings of terror that would send my heart hurtling into my stomach. Nowadays when decisions come to me with lightning speed I remember with wondering joy the old days when it was almost impossible to decide whether to cook rice or potatoes for dinner; when I would stand in the middle of the kitchen floor, head in hands, in an agony of indecision, trying to start the faltering battery of my mind.

Was I crazy in those old days? By no means! And no more are you, those of you who read this. Your emotional tone has dropped too low, that is all. Why? Weariness. Exhaustion from too much tension in your business or from the constant confusion of house and children or from the strain of holding down the bitter memories of the past or from the battle of the soul against anger and resentment—or from all of these.

Then what shall one do? Rest? That is good but not good enough, for one comes back from vacation and again plunges into turmoil. Then shall one seek to understand oneself and to correct all those matters within one's soul and within one's life that have bound one with chains? There are times when this is possible, but there are other times when it is not. One in the condition which I call mental depression—a condition of such darkness that the pilot light of the soul seems to have gone out—cannot deal alone with the haunting specters of the past. Countless thousands today go to doctors of the mind, and happy are those who have a wise counselor and who can afford to pay him. But far more thousands of thousands cannot avail themselves of professional help and one hopes they will never need to do so. For there are other ways.

One other way is to seek and find the nonprofessional help of a person powerful in prayer and skilled in the understanding of the mind. Such a person can instantly turn on the light in the darkness, and this I know right well, for it has happened to me not once but twice. The first time the change that took place in me through the simple prayer of faith was comparable to the change that takes place in a gas stove when one lights a pilot light that had gone out. This change did not automatically solve all my problems any more than the lighting of the pilot light automatically cooks one's dinner. But the light was there. The power to think and, even more important, to feel had returned. And from that light one could light all the burners, one after another, and could learn to cook with them.

For some thirty years the light stayed on, burning now brighter, now lower. Then there came a time when the pressure of life and its sorrows once more dimmed the light. This time, however, the light did not go out, for I had learned how to feed and to tend it in ways that I shall shortly describe. Indeed, I did not realize that it was once more burning low. I knew that the sorrows of life had increased upon me, but assumed that this was the inevitable result of age and of the tensions of my life. But the Lord sent to me someone who saw my need more clearly than I did, who insisted upon praying for me with faith and vigor, and who quite without any co-operation from me turned on the flame of the spirit with a fire that burned more deeply and more brightly than ever before.

As it happened, both who prayed for me at these different times were ministers.

Therefore take courage. This is not a battle you must fight alone. There is a power that watches over you whether you know it or not. There is the Creator who made you and who therefore cares—as every creator cares for the thing he makes. Being a creator, however, and not a magician or despot, He has given you the wide range of free will and therefore He cannot, or will not, overrule your own power of choice. If you are far away from Him then, you can choose to come back and at least to be near enough to Him so that He can help you.

In *The Healing Light* I described the prayer of the minister for the healing of a child's illness—the prayer which first opened my mind to the possibility of a direct intervention of God's power. For, like so many who walk only in the dim light of their own feeble minds, I believed that God no longer "manipulated" His creation; in other words, that creation had ceased. I did not know that even the flaming stars grow old and die and the Creator throws out other balls of fire, inconceivably and gloriously vast, to shine and whirl for aeons in the illimitable deep of the far sky. I did not know that the Creator forever broods over His creation, His arm still strong to save and to re-create, and that He intervenes directly when the need and the faith of man make it possible for Him to do so. He is still able to "manipulate"—to perform, to act, to work His works of salvation of the soul of man and of the soul of this little planet earth!

The first minister's prayer for my baby opened my mind to the possibility of physical healing. But my own need was for the healing of the soul and I did not dare go to the minister and ask for this healing lest it fail. Those of you whose hearts are burdened over-much will recognize this unwillingness to try the very thing that may save you. It is quite a sensible hesitation, really. We have the burden of life adjusted so that at least we can carry it, albeit heavily and with much labor and sorrow. What if for a moment we dare to put it down and it is not, after all, taken away, and we have not the strength to lift it again?

For a whole year I hesitated, lacking the energy to make the decision. Meanwhile the Creator who had sent His minister to me waited for a chance to reach my faltering soul. He found that chance at the communion rail. For although church then meant nothing to me, nevertheless from life-long habit and training I was there every Sunday morning, and it was this faithful churchgoing that saved my life. For on that morning God found a way to reach me. It was as if the clouds over my mind parted for a second and a command came to me: a voice that said, "Go and see that minister."

I have explained why I waited for a whole year. But why did God wait? Why did He not speak to me sooner, saying, "Go and be healed"? I have no doubt that He did, and that I did not hear Him. Alas, He has been so bold as to give us little blind ones free will that we may play havoc upon this earth! And yet perhaps one should not say "alas" but "Alleluia." For possibly He knows what He is about. And perchance it is through the ordered use of our own free will that the Kingdom will come at last. If it had been ten years later and someone had come to that church in need of healing of the soul he would not have had to wait during another year of sorrows. For there would have been many in that church praying for the Presence of the Creator to reach those in need and to heal them. Possibly on this Sunday those near me at the communion rail were Christians sufficiently in love and charity with their fellow men to be open to God and to make a highway for Him into the wilderness of my soul.

Therefore I speak out of my own heart when I suggest first of all that if we have given Him up in despair, we may once more take courage and come near to Him in His church, renewing those acts of loyalty that we had once felt to be our duty and had abandoned. I suggest also that we pray for the right person to come into our lives and help us. This is by no means so difficult as it was thirty years ago. For while I no longer do this work myself, I have taught and am teaching many others so to pray. And all over the world people are finding out the power of God and teaching it.

In the meantime however, there are ways, other than churchgoing, by which we may be able to help ourselves.

These ways are precisely contrary to the usual suggestions infuriatingly given by those who know nothing. "Come on, snap out of it," they say. "Be yourself!" Anything more asinine than this remark would be impossible to imagine. As if we could be ourselves merely by deciding to be ourselves! One cannot control the emotions of the deep mind simply by an act of will power. It is as stupid as saying to someone with two broken legs, "Come now, snap out of it! A brisk walk around the block—that is what you need!"

Moreover, the implication is that the mental depressive is merely neurotic. But mental depressives are not necessarily neurotics. The difference between neurotics and psychotics has been thus somewhat humorously defined by a psychiatrist friend of mine: "A psychotic says, 'Two plus two equals five,' and a neurotic says, 'Two plus two equals four and I *just can't stand it!*'" The neurotic is often an habitual complainer. The mental depressive is usually one who has refrained from complaining; who has put himself under such long and rigid control that he is worn out from the effort. To suggest further effort is useless. Another bit of spurious good advice is, "You must count your blessings." So I would do, saying to myself, "I have a fine husband and three lovely children and a comfortable home and no great financial problem. . . . There's no reason why I should feel this way. But I still do feel this way, so I must be going crazy!" I rule out, therefore, the stiffening of one's will and the counting of blessings.

Above all things, I do not suggest self-analysis. With

the help of a wise counselor one may be able to face the depths of the darkness above which one hangs by a thread. But alone the mental depressive cannot do this. He is climbing the steep cliff of life and is barely holding on by keeping his eyes firmly upon the next step, the next handhold on the ascent. It would be cruel for a well-meaning friend to say, "But look below! Such depths! Don't you see what an abyss you are hanging over? You might fall!" I would say, "Do not look!"

What, then, can one do to find life and peace? First of all I suggest that one rest upon the beauty of this world.

There is always the earth whence one came. There is always the old sea mother. There are the clouds and the far skies and the birds that fly within them. There are the little animals who run and frisk upon the earth. There is the sun pouring out life and light upon us. All these God made and He made them out of Himself, for there was no other source of life except Himself. "Let there be light," said the Creator in those unimaginable aeons when there was only darkness upon the face of the deep. And out of the darkness the light appeared. During all that first Day the light intensified, shifting and moving and changing its form. Not from sun or moon or stars did that light appear, for they had not as yet been created. So says the Bible with that amazing inspiration which, when considered with a modicum of common sense and even the smallest knowledge of modern science, is breath-taking truth. Whence, then, came that light? Whence but from God Himself? And what was that light from which all things evolved but the light of creativity, the very life-force existing in a radiation of an energy akin to the light one sees with the eyes, but existing at a higher rate of vibration? Before there were any living creatures to fly and run in that light, it brought forth the earth and the seas and plants upon the earth, each one having its seed within itself. So says the Bible and so say the sciences concerning earth and heavens. And before there were any human beings either to worship God or to defy Him, there were brought forth living creatures in the sea and on the land and in the sky. So says the Bible and so says science. *The simplest and oldest way, then, in which God manifests Himself is not through people but through and in the earth itself.*

And He still speaks to us through the earth and the sea, the birds of the air and the little living creatures upon the earth, if we can but quiet ourselves to listen.

There was a time long before I knew the healing power of God when I lay in a hospital so very ill that the desire for life had left me. The Lord spoke to me and brought back to me an interest in life and so the desire to live. He spoke through a gray squirrel who ran along the telegraph wire outside the hospital window. As I watched that tiny creature with its grace and beauty, I began to recover.

Years later there was a time when I greatly desired and needed a new inflow of God's Holy Spirit. I did not know what I needed. In those days no one had ever told me that the same baptism of Fire that came upon the apostles at Pentecost is still available to us today.

On a cold October morning I rowed across a small

lake and found an isolated point of rock overhung with pine trees. There I lay upon the pine needles with the warmth of the sun soaking into me. The wind breathed through the pine trees and a few late birds fluttered silently among them, their songs laid away for the winter. I prayed for God's life to reach me through the rays of the sun. And even though I did not know the Holy Spirit, the Spirit of God entered in a way so defying understanding that I have never before tried to explain it. Nor can I explain it now. I can only say that for a split second I lived consciously and awarely in the bliss of eternity. I saw nothing and I heard nothing, but I was so enwrapped and interpenetrated by the bliss of light that I thought, "If this doesn't stop I shall die!" And again I thought, "But I don't want it to stop." It ceased, and I have no way of measuring the time of it, for I was living beyond time. But the holy fire burned within my head for some fourteen days. I did not know then that it was the baptism of the Holy Ghost ("He shall baptize you with the Holy Ghost, and with fire") and not knowing, not understanding, I was unable to appropriate those various gifts of the Spirit that later came to me. But no experience ever equaled in bliss this baptism of pure light and power that came to me from God, not through the medium of man counseling and praying with me, but through the sun and the waters of the lake and the wind in the pine trees.

Understand now that this did not come the first time that I sought God in His surrounding world, nor the second. Nor am I saying that one can duplicate such an experience. But I am saying that there is comfort to be found in the very earth itself and in the creatures that live upon it. And I seriously suggest to mental depressives that they put themselves in the way of receiving this life. Those who live in the country can wander at will upon the consoling earth; they can lie on the grass in the summertime and immerse themselves in the coolness and the fragrance of it. They can walk beside the still waters and find peace. They can lean over an ancient wooden bridge and watch the dance of a millstream and make no effort to pray or even to think, and a forgotten feeling will begin to move and to dance within their souls. They can go down to the roaring sea and shed tears of joy as that immemorial mother awakens in them submerged memories that are race memories and not their own, and that beat with the very pulsebeat of the ages.

Even those who live in cities can find some park— some garden—maybe some bit of earth that is their own.

This is not a cure-all, but it can be, to some people at least, a beginning.

I once heard a minister say, "A candle gives out two kinds of light. One is the light that you see and another is an infrared glow that you cannot see. Moreover, this second kind of light is given forth not only from the flame but *from the candle itself*. And not only a candle but every created thing gives forth this light. Even a rock emanates an invisible energy, an infrared light—the light of the Creator shining through His creation."

"But I don't like nature," some of you may say. "Bees and birds and so on don't appeal to me."

Well, nature likes you whether you like nature or not. However, if you close your mind to finding help in beauty, then your mind is closed. Conversely, if reading these few words serves to open your mind even a little bit, then may that small opening ever increase as you walk through it into joy!

There are those who are more interested in another aspect of the creativity of God upon this planet. Things that grow and live of themselves, with little or no help from man, do not sufficiently challenge the intelligence. They prefer to be themselves creators, making living things out of words and paint, out of wires and tubes and metal and wood. These also can draw nearer to God by making Him a partner in their creative enterprise, whatever it may be. For God has chosen to make a world that is not static, but that has the principle of creativity built into it; each living thing having, in the words of Genesis, its seed within itself. (Gen. 1:11.) Is God then content with leaving the woods as they are, the fields untrodden and the brooks unbridged? There was a time when I so envisioned God, and felt vaguely apologetic at the efforts of man, often crude and distressful, to improve upon God's creation. But now I know that God wants man to improve upon His creation. Man's work upon this earth is merely the continuation of the plan of God, wherein nothing remains unchanged but all grows and develops from one stage to another. Indeed it seems at times as though God rested from His work of creation after He made man, waiting and watching to see how man would get on with it. "And God . . . rested on the seventh day. . . ." (Gen. 2:2.)

It is the very plan and intention of God, then, that man created upon this earth shall continue to create. The principle of creativity carried out in fertilizer factories and power plants, in suspension bridges and schools and airplanes and automobiles is of interest to God just as the efforts of nature to bring forth dinosaurs, since discarded in favor of more practical forms of life, are of interest to God. God therefore can be a partner and helper in any honest work or play. For play also is creative: the evolving of systems of thinking and acting that stimulate thought and life.

If anyone doubts this, considering it an unworthy female conception and too frivolous for serious consideration, let him read *The Phenomenon of Man* and *The Divine Milieu* by that great anthropologist and prehistorian, Pierre Teilhard de Chardin. And let him remember that the man who wrote these books was a Jesuit priest. His contemplation of the work of God through nature and through man is neither feminine nor frivolous, and his statements of the worth to God of all endeavor of the human mind is deeply consoling.

Therefore my second suggestion for drawing near to God that He may heal the soul is: make God a partner in some kind of creative activity.

But *how* can you draw near to God even through creative activity when He is so far away?

I can hear you saying, "Yes, but I can't. I have tried and tried and I can't find God."

I know. Therefore I am not going to urge you to try to find God. I am going to make some very simple suggestions that will help you put yourself in the way of God so that *He can find you.*

God is looking for you. He loves you. But He must have a voice through which to speak and the voices of men are apt to be too vigorous and lacking in understanding. Put yourself where God can find you—expose yourself to Him, as it were, like exposing a film so that the sunlight can print a picture on it.

For instance, I had a little plot of ground back of the parish house that I claimed as my own. I did not know that God spoke to me in a very gentle voice as I dug in the dirt and planted seeds or as I sat on the grass and watched the sparrows hopping about on the parish-house roof. But I would feel a tiny bit of comfort. It was easier to feel love for my flowers than for people. I think it was love. At least it was a comfortable feeling. Yes, I know. You are thinking, "I don't really love anybody—not even my husband [or my wife] and my children—but I must never never let anybody know it—it's too awful!" I know, because that was what I used to think. But the love was there all the time, underneath. It was only that my feeling-ability had dropped so low that I could not feel it. It was there! It was not gone. Neither is yours. Yes, of course, there are some people you hate—who doesn't, until he gets over being human? (One of these days you will get over being human, but that will take a long time, so do not worry about it now.)

You see, God is actually *in* the flowers and the growing grass and all the little chirping, singing things. He made everything out of Himself and somehow He put a part of Himself into everything. Oh, not His whole self! You don't want to see His whole self, do you? It would scare you to death. But if you will just go out of doors for a while every day, finding yourself a project so as to have an excuse for going out, it will help God to hold on to you until more direct help comes. It will be like a life preserver holding you up until somebody pulls you out.

But what if you live in a city? Well, even a city has bits of grass here and there and sparrows hopping in the sun. . . .

And shall you try to think about God while you walk or hit a golf ball or transplant zinnias? Oh, no. That would be too tiring. Just think about the golf ball or the zinnias or the sun on the rooftops.

Now if you hit a golf ball or transplant zinnias, actually you are exposing yourself to God in two ways because you are *creating*. You are creating a garden or a good style in golf. Of course in a preachy kind of way I could say that you are also creating while you are washing dishes or selling shoes, but it probably takes all the energy you have at the moment just to wash dishes or sell shoes without trying to figure out how you are thereby creating a home or a business. Until you become so filled with the joy of the Lord that you can find joy in everything, it is no fun to wash dishes or sell shoes. But it is easy to see that you are making a garden or that you are improving your swing in golf. It is fun. Real creativity is fun.

However, you cannot be out of doors swinging at golf balls every day. And some people don't like out-of-doors games or work, but prefer to go out merely to sit in the sun or walk or drive.

Therefore, my second suggestion is that you do whatever you best *like* to do for at least half an hour a day. What did you like to do before you sank beneath the burden of life? Knit? Make bookshelves and bird-houses and things like that? Take part in plays? Go fishing? Well, do whatever it was.

Watching television does not work in the same way. It can be very nice to pass the time and to relax you, but if you watch it very much you grow stale inside because it is too passive. You are not creating, only observing. In fact, if I were you I would not turn on and leave on any noisemaker, for it distracts your mind which otherwise might brood subconsciously on your creativity and come up delightedly with a new idea for crewel embroidery or trout flies.

Of course when you take time every day for a bit of creativity (fun-creativity) some people may think you are queer. "Why do you chase off and play golf when your house is at sixes and sevens?" So what? They think you are queer, anyway. They simply don't understand.

These suggestions will help you to keep afloat, until, perhaps, you learn to tread the deep water and to find your own way to the shore. But I also hope that some of you will be spared this long struggle; that someone will leap into the water after you and bring you immediately into safety.

For just that purpose I am spending the final stage of my life in training those who are well and sound of mind to do this work. Many ministers have come to the Schools of Pastoral Care that my husband and I started ten years ago. Now there are doctors and psychiatrists who dare add to their learned skills the simple ways of prayer. There are lay people like myself who have learned to understand and to practice prayer for the healing of the deep mind. It is my prayer that they will find you!

A friend of mine once met a woman in very deep depression, so much so that she was persecuted by a homicidal mania. Her unreasoning desire to kill was almost out of control. Yet she was to all appearances placid and sweet!

"You look unhappy," said my friend, while buying a dress from her. "I think I can help you. Will you come to see me?"

And help the woman she did, by the prayer of faith with the laying on of hands, and by teaching her how to pray. The troubled one was led, later on, to a wise counselor who gave the advice that my friend would not have taken upon herself to give. But my friend had leaped into the deep waters and had pulled her out of them, else that woman might have drowned before other help came.

I believe that if you will keep yourself open and

available to God, He will send you to the right person or send the right person to you at the right time.

In the meantime, there is an ever-increasing current and volume of prayer going forth to you. Many who have learned the power of prayer give themselves to the work of intercession not only for those whom they know but also for those whom they do not know. Indeed such intercessions as these are incorporated into the life of some churches and have been from the beginning. But, alas, if they are said without faith then there is little power to save in all these prayers. Nevertheless, the prayers are there—a framework to hold the reality of faith as soon as it is brought forth from the obscurity with which the years have veiled it.

I need hardly tell you that I am one of those who pray for you. It is no longer possible for me to do this work individually, person to person, for the field has grown too wide. The Lord has therefore guided me to a broader and more subtle way of prayer. It baffles me in a way, because I cannot tell what my spirit does and whither it goes. But that it does travel and that God does work through my spiritual body even when my mind is quite unaware of it, becomes more and more apparent.

Therefore, simply call in your mind to me, or to someone else as a human channel for the love of Christ.

2

To Those Who Care

THOSE WHO WALK IN DARKNESS WILL UNDERSTAND THE
simple directions given in the preceding chapter, or
even if they do not understand, will still be willing to
try them. But some of you who read this book may be
wondering: "Why don't these people in trouble simply
go to Jesus Christ? Should they not receive their help
directly from Him instead of from trees and birds and
playing the piano and carpentering?" Of course they
should if they were well enough in soul. There was
once a man who was carried to Jesus by four friends.
He would have gone to Jesus alone if he had been able
to do so, but at the time he could not walk. It is to
such as he that I have been speaking. May you who do
not know the meaning of mental depression thank
God that you have never had to walk in darkness, eyes
bound from seeing and ears from hearing. But in your
mercy, understand. These people cannot go to Jesus

unless you carry them into His presence. The best they can do without a healer is to find peace through the silent voices of the stars and of the stones and of the humble grass and the small creatures that live in it; and to find life through creating life by God's help with any tool that is theirs to use, their ability to sing or to polish furniture, to plant flowers or to plan businesses.

This is a slow way of coming to life. It is a beginning, but it is not an end. True. In addition, their souls need a healer. They need friends to carry them to Jesus in the strong arms of faith. They need shepherds to lead them beside the still waters.

And it may be you, my friend—it may be you whom the Lord broods over, saying, "Feed My lambs." Therefore I now write to you: to you who are willing to obey the Lord and to seek and to save those who are lost; or to those of you who simply have a friend whom you would like to help. You who have been reading for your own help may omit this chapter. Or, if you prefer to read on, remember that it is not written for you but for your helper. Remember this also: forbear to judge that helper if he does not follow the precise pattern indicated. He may know a better pattern, one more suited to his own nature and abilities. What follows is not meant to be absolute, but only to give suggestions gleaned from my own experience. Those who read may use what seems to them usable and forget the rest.

The first step is to know what person needs prayer for the healing of the soul and not to limit our interests to our family and friends. We want to help our friends, yes. But there are sure to be others—not our friends except as all God's children are our friends—who have an even greater need. And it is often easier to help a comparative stranger than to minister to a friend.

How shall we find these comparative strangers? If we are willing to obey Our Lord, we will find them. We will be moved with compassion even as Jesus was moved with compassion. (Matt. 14:14.) For instance, in Honolulu a tiny Japanese hairdresser told me with great delight of her healing prayers for her customers. "I can see when they are troubled!" she said, waving her scissors in the air to the electrification of the other beauty-seeking females. "We Orientals have an advantage over you Occidentals—we can *see* the dark spirits!"

I do not know just how the hairdresser "saw" the inner darkness of her customers, but I know how I see it: simply by looking upon the person with the eyes of understanding.

I have mentioned the prayer-healing of a woman in a depression verging on homicidal mania. Her helper, you remember, said to her while trying on a dress in a shop, "You look unhappy. I think I can help you."

First of all, the helper *saw*. Second, she spoke with that straightforward and unsmiling approach which wins the heart of the suffering one. She did not say, "God can help you," which would probably have aroused cynicism and suspicion. She simply said, "I can help you." This matter of the direct and personal approach is very important. Ministers particularly love to say, "God can help you." Please do not say it! No matter how sincere you are, it sounds to the other person like the hackneyed professional approach which they have come to distrust, because for years they have cried out for God to help them and He has not done so. Say *I* can help you." You do not at this moment have time to be humble. True humility consists, in any case, in caring so much for another that you do not think of yourself at all; and the question of whether or not you are speaking with due modesty simply does not enter your mind. The moment one considers one's own humility one is not humble.

It is also of great importance to speak to depressed persons with a straight face, giving them the honor of taking them seriously. Here again a temptation enters in: the temptation to try to lift their spirits by beaming and smiling and gamboling about in a spurious gayety. I assure you that the mental depressive cannot feel joyful merely because you grin and slap him on the back. He has had too much of this kind of treatment and it leaves him bleakly staring, all the more depressed because he knows that he cannot enter into your cheer nor respond to your joy. So this oversimplified method of tryi. g to cheer him by cheerfulness tells him that you are far outside of his trouble—that you neither see him nor hear him.

"*I* can help you." That is something new. It suggests not only that you have hope but that you care. Thus you begin to establish a rapport between the two of you. You may need to urge a bit before this one will come to see you, but I beseech you to urge. The one who most needs help may be too afraid to ask for it.

It will be best, however, if you can persuade the sufferer to come to you; best if you do not have to pursue him to his home. The act of faith in taking a step toward you is in itself a help, as is the privacy that you will be able to afford him in living room or study.

What shall you do then, when he comes to see you? One's first effort in all healing is the effort of arousing in the other person the faith to be healed. In physical healing one does this by a joyous explanation of God's healing power. But in the case of the mental depressive I have not found that the best way. You are still too far outside his trouble. Therefore I usually begin by telling all the worst things I can think of about myself, not with the idea of seeking sympathy or help, but in order to show that I understand through experience. "You look as though you feel the way I used to feel," I begin. "It was awful! I was afraid all day and all night. I didn't know what I was afraid of, I was just afraid. I didn't dare go near an upstairs window for fear I'd jump out of it. Every time I used a knife in the kitchen ——"

"Why I'm that way too!" the other person may say in great amazement.

"Of course," one continues serenely. "It's one of the symptoms. And the darnedest thoughts used to troop through my head—they weren't even nice, let alone sensible ——"

"Yes!" breathes the lost one.

"Then I would sometimes try to take my mind off my troubles by going to a movie or watching television, and I'd feel better for a little while. But afterwards my heart would drop back into my stomach so that I wondered whether it was easier just not to try."

"Oh, yes!" And my friend heaves a deep sigh of comfort. "But everybody says, 'Come on, snap out of it—you must make an effort. . . .'"

"And making an effort only pushes you farther in, as though you were sinking in quicksand."

"But how did you get over it?" (I do not need to tell this person that I did get over it.)

"There are some simple things I learned that helped me. But, first of all, someone else who knew the way pulled me out. He laid his hands on me and prayed for me. I know that sounds silly, but that's what he did and it worked. And I can do that too. That's why I wanted you to come to see me. Do you mind if I try?"

As one person said to me at this point, "Lady, I'll believe anything you say and do anything you tell me to do, because you're the only person who has known how I feel inside my own mind."

However, the sufferer may say, "But I don't have any faith."

Now God be thanked that the one who is strong can lift up the one who is weak—that we can interpose our own faith for the faithlessness of another! "That's all right," I respond. "I can have faith for you. Of course you can't have it for yourself. Your mind is too tired to make that effort."

But did not Jesus require faith of all? No. If you will search the Scriptures you will see that Jesus did not demand faith of one whose mind was darkened or disturbed. He did not require faith of Jairus's daughter or the centurion's son or the maniac of Gadara. He took the power of God in His own hands and *spoke for them* the word of faith.

And so can we, pouring into this person the light and life of God through our own minds and bodies. For this purpose the laying on of hands in the sacramental way, upon the head, is most valuable. A minister need make no explanation of this ministerial gesture. It is expected of him by his people. Even though his church may have forgotten and lost the original churchly method of the laying on of hands in prayer, this is so simple and natural an act that the one for whom he prays will not think it strange. Most people instinctively look upon their minister as a mediator between them and God. So he is called and set apart to be, and so they desire him to be. They do not need a pal or a playfellow. They need a mediator. Deep in their hearts they know this, no matter what the regulations of their church may say. And when the need is great, they will accept it without question. I myself, not being a minister, say a word of explanation: "I'd like to stand behind you if you don't mind, and just put my hands on your head. It works better that way." I do not try to explain the actual radiation of life and light that comes through the human being, as light shines through the light bulb, for their minds are too confused to understand. I do not explain that as my words reach their conscious minds, so God's words flow through my body and my hands into their bodies and reach the unconscious mind that is the storehouse of the emotions. Nor do I need to remind myself of this. I say a prayer of the utmost simplicity. I ask Our Lord to come into the mind and heal it and restore the original personality. And I make in words little pictures of thankful expectance that He *is* thus entering and healing the soul. Why should I not give thanks? Is not the healing of the soul the very purpose of His holy sacrifice on Calvary? Is it not, then, His will and the will of the Father? What could stop it? He often heals bodies as well as souls, and I know that He longs to do so always. But under the grievous circumstances of this life, sin being prevalent and the Kingdom of God being so very far away from the world around us, there are times when healing of body fails. But the healing of the soul never fails. And even if the person were to die within twenty-four hours, it is of eternal value that he go with a soul lit by the light of the Lord rather than with a soul caught in the power of darkness. Therefore I give thanks again and again so that the inner mind may grasp this truth and act upon it. I make word pictures of the sufferer as she will be when the real one comes forth, and thank the Lord for those pictures. "Thank You, Lord," I say, "She will wake up, like waking up out of a bad dream, and will look around the world and see that it is beautiful. She will look at her children and see what fun they are. She will be able to enjoy them again, instead of just worrying about them. She will begin to take an interest in other people and in church work and. . . ." But surely I need not go on.

The prayer being over, I bring the interview to an end as quickly as possible lest the effects of the prayer be dissipated by scattered words.

"Don't look into yourself to see how this is working," I say. "When you plant a seed, you don't keep pulling it up to see whether it is growing roots. This is the seed of a new life planted in you and it is bound to grow."

Many a time even while saying this you can see in the eyes of the one once lost the light of a new life. Even so, do not speak of it lest your too-quick words frighten the deep mind.

Sometimes the found one, once lost, will say (quite forgetting that she or he had no faith), "How shall I pray for myself?"

Whereupon I respond, "Don't! You would just get confused. For a little while, let me carry the burden for you. And call me up when you'd like to see me again."

In a sense, you do carry the burden. You pray for that person daily until he or she is able to pray. But let it be as light as possible, this carrying; remind yourself that the final responsibility is on His shoulders, not on yours, lest you be overwhelmed with troubles not your own and so lose power. Remember the words of the Lord Jesus when He said, "He that would come after me, let him take up his cross and follow me." What is our cross? The enduring of selfish illnesses because we are too lazy to make the spiritual effort of overcoming them? Then what is our cross? The dark night of the soul that we may hug it to ourselves and concern ourselves world without end merely with the triviality of ourselves? Then what is our cross? Surely this: that those who for the moment are strong shall help to bear the burdens of those who are weak. "Bear ye one another's burdens and so fulfill the law of Christ."

So in prayer we lift this burden from the other one, and then we give it to Him who alone can bear all our burdens. We do not fall again into depression! God forbid! Would He desire that we should lose our joy and so lose our power? Not so. But we do momentarily feel a sense of virtue going out of us as even Our Lord felt it (Mark 5:30); we do sense at times physical strain and weariness and the need to walk more closely with Him.

How long do we pray for this person who so needs Christ? And how often do we see him? There is no rule. But we would naturally desire to see him more than once. I do not say to him on his next interview, "But you must accept the fact that God has healed you." Nonsense! That would be requiring him to make a leap of faith that he is not able to make. For this next interview I gird myself carefully with faith; much may be required of me. Usually the person comes to report a new life and a new freedom, perhaps adding, "But it is dimming down a little bit." Occasionally, however, he will say, "I don't feel any better! In fact I think I feel *worse!*" One must take this without wincing. One must never, never show fear or disappointment in one's face or voice—but never! So when this (fortunately) rare remark is made, what shall one say? Something like this:

"Well, let's see. How did you feel the first day or two?"

"I seemed to be better for two or three days . . ."

"All right, that shows that there is a power and it does work. We must figure how to keep at it so that you don't collapse so soon. Suppose we try it again. We can take God's light into us more than once, you know, just as we can take more than one pill. And this time, come back on the third day so that we can catch it before you swing down again."

It is still too soon to deal with the person's sins and problems, but that time will come. And when it comes from the person, then it is safe.

"I felt like a new person," someone may say. "And then, all of a sudden, that wonderful feeling went away from me."

"What happened just before it went away?"

"Well, my husband and I—it was before breakfast and I guess we were in a bad mood . . ."

And there you have it, the first lesson in the Christian life: forgiveness.

Thus the prayer relationship passes inevitably into a counseling or teaching relationship. Nor are the two from the beginning in any way alien to each other. The one who prays imparts understanding whether he knows it or not. The one who counsels in any kind of Christian context emanates a spiritual power whether he knows it or not.

At this point another question rears its perplexing head; namely, the question of time. For how long must one carry this newborn soul lest it fall into the slough of despond? The minister (and by this I mean the one who ministers God's power, whether ordained or not) may feel burdened and harassed, may wish to slip out of further responsibility or involvement, yet the one thing he must not do is to abruptly terminate his healing relationship in such a way that the one for whom he prays feels rejected. But he cannot forever carry this person on his back like an old man of the sea!

In my own experience this problem took care of itself, first of all in teaching those whom I helped how to pray for others. It is surprising how soon this can be done. The usual question after some three interviews is, "Can I help others as I have been helped?" And my answer is always "Yes." Even when the person says, "But I'm far from well myself," my answer is still "Yes." It is much easier to pray objectively for others than to pray subjectively for oneself. And in the very act of praying the prayer of faith for others, one is apt to extrovert some of one's own trouble and to open a window in the soul through which God's light can shine. I do this teaching first alone and casually, as questions arise, and then, later, in a group or class.

To the question, "When can I see you again?" I reply, "Come to my Bible class. There a lot of us learn together about the prayer of faith and the way of life."

"But I'd rather see you alone!"

"I'm sorry, but with three children and housework and writing, I don't have time. But really, in the long run, you'll find that you get much more from the Bible class than from me popping in to pray with you."

I realize that many people do not know enough about the Bible to teach that holy book. Here I have a great advantage through no merit of my own, for in the mission field in China I absorbed the Scriptures from infancy along with my Borden's condensed milk. I cannot remember the time when I did not study one chapter of the Bible and memorize certain verses every day. Nothing in my life has been of more value than this weaving of the words of life into my subconscious. However, I did not depend upon this childhood knowledge alone in teaching the Bible, but hied me to my husband's study and bore home certain weighty tomes of commentaries and Bible dictionaries and concordances. I opened the book at Genesis 1:1 and pursued it all the way to Rev. 22:21. "How long did that course in the Bible take you?" someone asked me. And I replied quite truthfully, "Eighteen years." True, the membership of the class changed but I continued teaching!

We did not study the Bible from the critical point of view, though I could not help pointing out the increasing agreement between the Bible and the most modern findings of science. We did not concern ourselves with the possibility of two Isaiahs and any number of St. Johns, but rather with the essential truth concerning God and man and the way of life that comes through these inspired pages, sometimes in one shaft of light amid great darkness, sometimes in floods of light that the world has not yet begun to see.

"But I have never studied the Bible in that way!" most of you are thinking.

What of it? The Bible is not locked, neither is it chained. As for the necessary commentaries, one can find them in libraries and religious bookstores. I would add only this: I do not swallow whole anything that I learn from a commentary or any other book until I have submitted it to the X-ray light of God's Holy Spirit. After my research upon the chapter for the day's lesson is done I read the chapter again very slowly in a spirit of prayer, saying, "Lord, I have done all I can with my conscious mind. Now please show me the deeper meaning of these words." And from the inner being there often flows a light illuminating the page as a flashlight illumines a path through a dark woods.

"All this is too much trouble," some of you are thinking. "Why can't I just take this mentally depressed person into my prayer group?"

For several reasons: first, anyone recovering from mental depression is seldom ready to take on other peoples' burdens in a prayer group. Not only is she herself apt to be overburdened and disturbed, but she (or, of course, he) is apt to distract the group. It is usually best therefore that the prayer group pray for this person rather than inviting her into their midst. It is for such reasons as this that I prefer the small private prayer group to the "organized" and announced one. Let there be two groups! A larger group open to all for study of the Bible or for "group therapy" if one is versed in that method, and a smaller and more intensive group of chosen people for intercessions.

Now all of this is pointed, obviously, to the step-by-step healing of the average sick soul. But it is impossible to standardize either God or man, and sometimes there takes place at the first prayer what can only be described as a resurrection. For instance, a young woman was brought to me by her sister just after she had taken the seventeenth shock treatment of a series of twenty. She had all her life been a depressive person for reasons which I still do not know. She had twice attempted suicide. She was also a serious diabetic. As she was obviously too disturbed for any kind of conversation, I simply talked and prayed with her in the manner described earlier and with absolutely no knowledge of the nature of her trouble. She sat immobile in the rocking chair in my living room and I said, "Stay here as long as you like. I'll go into the kitchen and start dinner."

After twenty minutes she came in. "What happened?" she said. "I couldn't move till now. Something was flowing all over me . . ."

She went home, still in a daze. The next day she called up to tell me that she was well. "I told the psychiatrist I did not need to come back," said she. "He didn't understand, and he was quite upset. Finally he said, 'Well, you've paid for the twenty shock treatments. You may as well come in and have the other three.' But I told him No. I was well and he could keep the money—I was not coming."

Time showed that she really was well. Furthermore she was a completely transformed personality and since then has started a prayer group of her own and has been the channel of healing for many people. Four years later she came to see me and said, "Today is my birthday."

"Congratulations!" said I in my Chinese way. "How old are you?"

"Four," she replied.

"*Four?*"

"Don't you remember it was four years ago today that I sat in your big chair and you prayed for me? That was my birthday. I had never really lived until then."

Her diabetes, while wonderfully controlled by insulin and diet so that she lives as a well woman, has not been actually healed. Why? I do not know. But I am thankful for the greater healing—the healing of her soul.

This story raises several questions. Do I advise people to give up their psychiatrists? No, I do not, any more than I would advise them to give up their medicine. But sometimes they themselves know when they no longer need this type of care, and when they do know it I rejoice—and usually I might say, their counselors also rejoice.

Second and more important, "What happened?" How could a deep-seated trouble be immediately healed through a simple prayer of faith for the healing of the soul?

In this manner: a person can have two areas of trouble, one in the circumstances of life and the other in the spirit itself. Two women can suffer the identical difficulties of, shall we say, an alcoholic father, a domineering mother, a runaway husband, and so on. Yet one can hold up her head and maintain herself while the other crumples completely. Why? Because in one the spirit lives and in the other the spirit has died—or, at least, is dormant. It is not functioning. So, whatever the human causes of depression may be, there is one sure universal cause—the inner light has gone out. What is this inner light? Oh, that I knew! The cloud of glory that we come trailing into this darkened world? The unconscious memory of that land from whence we came? The sense and feeling of the life that is immortal, we being mysteriously risen with Christ? I cannot say. But I know there is a focus and center of life within that illumines all our being, and when this light of life goes out, we are plunged into inner darkness. That is why the prayer of faith for the healing of the soul is really so simple. The primary cause of the trouble we *do* know. Therefore we are praying not in ignorance but in *sure knowledge* for the light of God to enter and awaken him that sleepeth, that he may rise from the dead and Christ may give him life.

3

The Fellowship of the Concerned

WHAT NEXT? WE HAVE SEEN A PERSON STRUGGLING OUT
of depression, trying to find the comfort of God in His
created universe and in the principle of creativity.
What, then, is his next step? Shall he now try to
analyze the causes of his emotional illness and to pray
for the healing of the soul? No, I do not think so. It is
still too soon. The wavering one might be dragged
back into introspection—into watching the wheels of
thought go around. There is nothing so deadly as this
to one coming out of depression. It is apt to lead to
that confusion which is the first step into despair.

Yet this person does need to learn how to pray, or,
in other words, to have an active interchange of
thoughts with God. I suggest therefore that he now
learn how to pray the prayer of faith for physical ills.
One can see the body. One can feel it. And one is not
so terrified, in praying for the healing of these small

ills, lest that prayer fail. What if it does? One can still live.

But, my wise readers are thinking, these disturbances in the body come from disturbances in the mind. Surely. Therefore any progress in healing the body will introduce hope and faith and strength into the mind as well, and, as faith increases, the deeper problems of life and personality can also be faced and healed.

The prayer of faith is not a magic formula, but is quite simply a prayer with a definite objective and with the belief that this definite need will be met. The mental depressive is apt to have migraine headaches, sinus trouble, indigestion, nightmares, dizziness, and a host of other small functional disturbances. Let him then choose one of these and try to connect it by faith with the power of God that heals. For no one is really healed until he has learned to make his own contact with the Healer.

The crux of the prayer of faith is this: *God's power is real.* The creativity of God sent forth when the Creator said in faith, "Let there be light," still radiates through His universe. This flow of energy has been put to use in all ages, from the savage dancing in the jungle to the modern man who teaches that all else save this power of God is error. I am not writing this book, however, for primitive people who create an atmosphere of faith by war paint and feathers and drums, though I look with respect upon these early efforts to contact a power that is real. Nor am I writing for those who already have a way of faith wrought by the denial of all that is not good—though upon these also I look with respect and indeed sometimes with envy, wishing that I could grasp their theory and seeing dimly that behind it there is an area of truth. But I cannot think after this pattern, for I am not of this nature. I am a graduate mental depressive and am too smashingly aware of the tragedy and horror of life to be able to look beyond it and say all is good.

How, then, shall I create in myself the atmosphere of faith: the feeling that God is answering my prayer? The method that I use is the training of the creative imagination.

This is difficult! Yes. But take courage, you who tend to depression: it has its good aspect. You will be less inclined to be led astray by too gullible a faith; to listen to the happy ones who chirp "All things are possible with God" and "Say a little prayer and forget it." Such people ignore the fact that while undoubtedly all things are possible with God, all things are not as yet possible with them. Their power is not as yet developed nor is their faith stabilized. They forget also that God does not work through magic but through the application of laws and of powers that He has created; and therefore one usually needs a continual and persistent application of prayer in order to keep the door open for the power that heals. Finally, they do not realize that no one lives alone and the entire race must rise to a higher awareness of God before all things that are possible with God become actual.

Therefore be content to walk slowly, for so your

journey will, in the end, lead you past dangers and into greater heights.

I suggest therefore that in the prayer of faith you do these things:

A. Choose which symptom or weakness you will pray about first and do not try to pray for all of them at once.

B. Form your prayer in words that suggest to the body the healed condition and not the continuing trouble. For every cell in the body has a rudimentary mind and will hear your words. For instance, I learned in praying for the healing of migraine headaches not to pray "Please don't let me have headaches any more" for the very word "headache" suggested headaches to the body-mind. (I learned also never to try to pray while actually suffering a headache, for the effort of prayer only made it worse. At such a time two aspirins and bed was better.) I worked out this form of prayer: "Come into me, O Lord, and heal the blood of the body so that it flows from head to foot in perfect order and harmony with no congestion anywhere." The headaches were not completely healed until years later when the memories were healed, but they became much better from the time that I began to pray this prayer once a day.

C. Make, in the imagination, a picture of the thing that you purpose in prayer. Hold this picture in the mind as much as possible, but lightly, as one plays a game. When, for a time, symptoms recur, bring the picture back to mind and speak consolingly to the body, saying in effect, "Never mind, here is the picture of what shall be and we are on our way to it." Do not scold the body. Understand that a healing of trouble such as this, brought on by the pressures of life, requires time. There is nothing to be frightened about if it does not take place all at once.

D. Give thanks to God that His power is entering and is working toward wholeness in the body in all ways best according to His will.

Yes, you give thanks before you see the healing. You say "Thank you" if a friend offers to do a favor for you. It is the natural and courteous thing, and it keeps the way open so that the favor can be done. Note, in my expression of thanks above, the use of the words "according to Thy will" rather than the words "If it be Thy will." All prayer is in essence an attempt to work out and establish what we believe to be God's will. When we go to a doctor (which we are also free to do, because prayer does not rule out medical care any more than it rules out the eating of food), we take for granted that it is right to seek healing—in other words that it is according to the will of God. So does the doctor or he would not be a doctor! But I do suggest the words "according to" instead of "if" because those words are strong words suggesting faith, whereas the word "if" is a weak word suggesting doubt.

Now to you ministers, ordained or not ordained, I suggest the necessity of teaching your people how to pray rather than trying to do all the praying for them. You can teach your mental depressive friends by direct instruction either individually or in a group. But why wait till people are depressed? You who have pulpits, what is to stop you from teaching these principles of the prayer of faith in your pulpits and in your confirmation classes, restating them in whatever words are most acceptable to your particular brand of churchmanship? Not only will this relieve you of much follow-up work in prayer but also it is more healthy for the individual souls of your people to learn God's power than merely to run to your study or to a healing service whenever they feel an ache or pain.

In addition to the obvious reason why this is more healthy—the growth in maturity of the soul—there is another reason which has to do with the connection of soul and body. If you try too vigorously to heal every tight spine and nervous stomach you may take away a certain transfer of tension that, for a while, the soul needs. Some people say with smug superiority that there are those who keep a symptom in the body on purpose so that they need not work out the spiritual cause of it. This would suggest that the conscious mind decides, "No, I'd rather have migraine headaches than learn to forgive." I maintain that this is not always the truth. There may be some who do feel thus, and if so, fine. Let them have migraine headaches. But with most people it is not so definitive as that. It is rather that the unconscious mind, knowing that this person is not yet able to face all the problems of life past and present, transfers part of the tension to the body. The body acts as a shock absorber. It helps the mind to carry the load by taking part of it and working it off in physical symptoms. If you are too insistent on healing these physical symptoms you may disturb this rapport of mind and body. But if you teach the person himself to pray, then the inner wisdom will work out the balance of soul and body—more slowly perhaps than you would like, but in a way that is more sure and safe.

Considering all these things, it is very distressing that some churches tend to seize upon the matter of healing prayer and claim that it should not be done except by ministers and in healing services.

How strange that human beings try to narrow and confine a Creator who cannot be narrowed and confined! How dismaying to find that already healing has become in some churches stylized, a matter of form and of routine: one gives a name to the prayer group or goes to the healing service and one has done one's Christian duty. Some ministers even teach that healing being the work of the church, no lay person should do it. What do they mean by this? For what is healing save prayer that the good Lord answers? Can any clergyman declare that no one may pray except himself? If he refers to the sacrament of Holy Unction or of the laying on of hands in a public service, well and good. That is truly the special work of the church just as the administering of Holy Communion is the work of the clergy. But do we not eat bread at our own tables for the needs of our bodies? And might we not even drink the juice of the grape?

We need the bread of life, which is the power of the Holy Spirit entering us for the health of soul and body, just as much as we need our daily physical bread. And the Holy Spirit, who is the giver of the gift of healing, simply cannot be circumscribed within the walls of a church. He cannot abide it and He will not, but will dim His power in any church that dares to claim Him as the exclusive tool of the clergy. For indeed the healing Spirit of God is in the wind and the sun and in the little creeping things upon the earth and is most certainly available to the one who prays with faith be he minister or layman, man, woman or child.

A friend from the deep South learned of the power of God to heal not from her minister but from the assistant garbage collector.

She noticed that Robert had not collected her garbage for several weeks. Finally, one day, she ran out to the street after Robert's assistant as he climbed into his truck.

"Oh, Mrs. Bob," he said. "Haven't you heard about Robert? Robert got a stevedore job down to the ship-yards and he fell and broke his back in three places."

And the assistant garbage collector called after her as he started his truck, "Mrs. Bob! My God can make a way where there ain't a way!"

"We ought to buy some cigars for Robert and go to see him," said my friend to her husband Bob later.

I expressed some surprise at her choice of a sickbed present. But my friend knew his tastes, and so she and her husband, complete with cigars, went to the hospital and found their Negro friend lying on his back in great distress.

"Mrs. Bob, they say they're going to put me in a cast all the way from my shoulders to my knees, and I just don't know how I can stand it!" groaned Robert.

"And I didn't know how he could stand it, either," said my friend, when telling me the story; "with the hot weather coming on—and no air conditioning in those days . . ."

So she went away to a conference on prayer, learned the prayer of faith, and threw her whole soul into praying for Robert.

On returning home she went immediately to call on Robert. As she slowed the car at the hospital entrance she saw him sitting in a chair on the porch. Amazed, she stopped the car and walked across the grass to him.

"Mrs. Bob, the Lord healed me and they don't need to put on no cast," said Robert.

Neither of them could utter another word. Both were silent, the tears running down their cheeks. But as my friend walked back to the car Robert called after her, "Mrs. Bob! My God can find a way where there ain't a way!"

And He had found it this time not through a church or through a sacrament but through a simple woman who loved her friends.

I was once traveling on the train from Washington to Philadelphia. I was very tired, having worked all day lecturing and praying for the sick (in private conferences as is my custom, not in a healing service). Ordinarily I would have curled up on the seat and slept. But I felt alert—or should I say alerted? I sat bolt upright and prayed.

The train stopped at Baltimore, then pulled itself together and drew slowly out of a tunnel between steep banks. There was a crash, an outcry, splinters of flying glass, and on the floor beneath the seat, a large stone. The window ahead of me had been broken by a stone hurled from the bank. My first thought was to thank God that I was unharmed. My second thought was, "What happened to that young man sitting in front of me?"

He lay drooped over the end of the seat and the blood from a gash in his forehead had already flowed in a thick stream down the length of two train seats and was spurting very fast. Clearly I had been planted there by the Lord to be the channel of healing for this man. I leaned over the back of the seat and put my hands beneath his head, this simple human touch making a channel between person and person and between God and man.

People rushed about trying to staunch the blood. The train stopped. The conductor leaped to a telephone beside the track and called ahead to Havre de Grace, an unscheduled stop, for an ambulance and a doctor to meet the train. Meanwhile the flow of blood had stopped. If anyone noticed me I simply said, "I'm supporting his head." But while supporting it I continued silently to pray the prayer of faith, asking for God's healing light to come into him and to completely and immediately heal the wound. I then gave thanks that it was so, expressing that thanks both in the word "Amen" and in the English translation of it which is "So it is." And I lent to the prayer the power of my imagination, seeing the wound healed.

In less than ten minutes the man regained consciousness and sat up, wanting to know what all the fuss was about.

"But I don't need a doctor and an ambulance," he insisted. "I'm all right. And I don't want to go to Havre de Grace, I want to go to Philadelphia!"

However, to Havre de Grace he went, the doctor and the ambulance being already on their way. He turned as he rose to leave the train and I saw the wound on his forehead. It was only a thin white line, like a scar some three weeks old. And he walked down the aisle tall and straight, quite alone and still protesting.

I have often wondered what he thought of this and, indeed, that is my reason for using this particular incident to illustrate a spontaneous and unsacramental prayer for healing. Someone who knows him might just possibly read this and say to him, "That sounds like your crazy story!"

I might point out that the Good Samaritan did not merely go his way and say, "I will present your case to the synagogue." It is good to have a church. But not every act of kindness can be deferred or there will be those who may die while waiting . . . and there may be others whose souls may wither and die for lack of direct action. It is good to have healing services and Communion services and fellowships of the concerned. But it is not enough. All life needs to be a fellowship of the concerned, for as God is concerned for all of us, so we need to be concerned one for another and to pray one for another that we may be healed, as the Bible bids us do.

The more that members of a church believe in prayer and in the power of the Holy Spirit, the more is healing freed for the services in that church. I was once in Christ Church St. Lawrence in Sydney, Australia, and after the healing service was asked to join informally in prayer with Father John Hope for a young woman with inoperable cancer. Frankly, I awaited this meeting in some dismay, picturing a bedraggled female crawling into church. This was not a very faithful picture, but I am only an ordinary person and my faith does not always shine brightly. However, when she walked in, erect and rosy cheeked and radiant, my heart leaped swiftly into faith. For she had been to many healing services and was almost completely healed. This was only to be a prayer for the establishment and maintenance of health. So I prayed, as once instructed by a doctor friend, that the body would from that time forth make only adult, normal cells (for cancer, the doctor had said, is a matter of the cells growing too rapidly, as in a child) and that if there were any undiscovered abnormal cells hiding in her, the power of the Holy Spirit would come in as a fire and burn them away.

But I knew in my heart that she did not need the prayer. She was already healed through the regular sacramental approach to healing carried on for thirty years by the great and gentle saint of the church, Father John Hope. That church was full of the power of the Lord! One felt it amid incense and candles (for Father John loved all these signs of God's presence) and one felt it even more through the love that pulsed through the church so that all were welcome there, not only those dressed in their Sunday best but also all Father John's friends from prison and reform school and the darkest alleys among the streets. This I know well, for I stepped over one of them in the vestibule, where he was quietly sleeping off his night's celebration. Nor did anyone think this "crook." The weather was balmy, the floor was warmly paved with love, and he was perfectly welcome among the more alert worshipers who knelt in the church. This church, due to the faithful work of the old priest (now retired), was full of salvation and of love.

But all churches are not so. And if healing comes to be regarded as just another gimmick or, I should more properly say, just another organized activity of the church, they will never become so.

Even a prayer group, I find to my dismay, can become destructive instead of creative. If the members of the prayer group consider themselves set apart, having a special experience of the Holy Spirit hidden from the rest of the congregation, then they do not unite—they divide. I can feel some of you thinking, "But this cannot be helped! We *do* have the Holy Spirit—and they don't."

Listen, my friends, the Holy Spirit can *have you* but He *cannot be had*. And if you try to hold this heavenly power to your little group—and if that group becomes the center of your religious life, so that the church services on Sunday morning are merely a form in which you tend to lose interest—then your group is already on the wane. Have you never wondered why such groups within a church are apt to start with joy and vigor and then to dim down and "peter out," the joy waning, the power fizzling into mere emotion and then fading away? The answer is not far to seek. The Holy Spirit is a power, an energy, the water of life—and when that power is not given forth to the whole congregation from whence the group sprang, when that energy is not used to awaken life within the Body of Christ, when the water of life is kept and hoarded rather than being freely expended, then the water stagnates, the energy is turned off, the power dwindles.

On my little farm in the hills of New England there is an old well that has been in use for more than a century. I have never tasted such delicious water, soft and sweet and ice-cold. However, when plumbing was installed in the old house it proved necessary to drill an artesian well. One day there was a thunderstorm and the electricity went off. Therefore the electric pump did not work. Therefore we had no water. So I thought, "It will be delightful to go and draw water out of that old well again!" And I joyfully went forth with bucket tied to rope. I pushed away the overhanging lilac boughs, shoved aside the rotted wooden top and let down the bucket. There was no water in the well—only mud!

When I next saw my plumber friend I said to him, "Austin, what happened to my old well? There's no water in it!"

"You haven't been using it, have you?" said Austin. "When you don't use it, the well gets all clogged up with its own silt. The more you use it, the more the water comes. And as it comes it tends to come clean."

"But we do use the power!" you are thinking.

Yes, for whom? For your special prayer projects—for your own. And do you go forth to seek and to save even these or do you merely sit comfortably praying in the Spirit?

Sorry, but it won't work that way: not for long.

God's power is an expanding power. It is in the very nature of creativity that it shall grow; that it shall go from one stage to another stage. When any tree or plant ceases growing, it has already begun to die.

Therefore one may begin in one's extremity praying only for one's own healing. One may continue by praying for a few friends. One may even add some unknown persons whose names are given to the prayer group. But the time will come when one is required by the Creator to expand this work, for its final purpose is no less than the bringing upon earth of the Kingdom of Heaven. And to those who belong to a church the next step is the extending of the power of God into the church for the benefit of the entire congregation, those who understand and those who do not understand.

This became, in years gone by, the greatest work of my prayer groups and of my Bible class. This work for the congregation was never announced. Many never knew why that church so increased in power that even to go into it lifted up the heart and strengthened the body. If we had made the work public, it would have lost power.

We went to church some ten minutes early in order

to pray for the presence of Jesus Christ to fill that church with His healing and redeeming love. When the minister entered, we prayed for him; not that he should do what we wanted him to do or believe what we wanted him to believe, but simply that God would pour out upon him His blessing and bring forth the highest potential of his being. Next we looked about the church to see whether there was anyone there whose face made us feel uncomfortable—in other words, anyone whom we did not like, of whom we disapproved, who had hurt us or who disapproved of us—and we prayed for that one. We did not deny that person's faults. We redeemed them through prayer. We asked the love of Christ to come into us and go through us into this person, healing the memories and bringing forth all that was good and lovely in his nature. Then we gave thanks as one does in the prayer of faith, and with inspired imagination we made in the mind a picture of that person transformed into the image of his real Christ-self and we rejoiced that this was so.

Inevitably our feeling about this person changed. Through our prayer we gave birth to his spirit; therefore he became to us a spiritual child and we brooded over him as a parent over a child, striving in prayer until the picture that we saw in the mind was accomplished. Moreover this person's feeling also changed!

"You know old Miss So-and-So," one of my friends would say. "She hasn't spoken to me for twenty years. Well, I prayed for her in church this morning, and she turned around on the steps and took both my hands and said 'Good morning' and was just lovely!"

Certainly. This woman did not know in her conscious mind that the love of Christ had gone forth to her through the prayer of her neighbor, but her unconscious knew it and responded with love. Of course! This is forgiveness—real forgiveness: giving the love of Christ to one who needs it.

Perhaps you are thinking, "But I have often prayed for such a person and it hasn't worked . . ."

Yes, but have you prayed *in church?* There you have them! They cannot escape you! They are quiet and attentive with their minds more or less open to God— and so you can sneak into the back door of the unconscious and they cannot keep you out! (You may miss a bit of the sermon in doing this, but the Lord will forgive you.)

After some years of this kind of prayer there was not so far as I know a quarrel of any kind in the church; not even a jealousy, not even a hate. Why should there have been? The prayers of the faithful in that church had healed the Body of Christ among them. Naturally!

Next we prayed for healing for certain individuals, often sharing our projects beforehand and sometimes making them our special intention for the Communion and receiving for them with prayer and fasting. *And all in secret.* (Matt. 6:6)

Finally we prayed for the healing power of the Lord to touch the mind and heart and body of any in that church who needed healing.

And it worked. The most wonderful healings that I

have ever known took place through the silent prayers of that prayer group in and among and through the whole congregation.

Healing is, after all, the work of the Holy Spirit and it is a group work. The Holy Spirit came first of all to a whole congregation—a hundred and twenty people praying together. And the more freely that water of healing life is poured out for the whole congregation, the more it fills the church. So the prayer group melts indistinguishably into the congregation and becomes a part of them. Thus it unites, it does not divide.

I need hardly add that as the group prays for and with the congregation, so the group also works with them, rejoicing in being members, doing their share in sewing circle or vestry, committees on church suppers and fairs, Sunday school or canvass. Every church activity in which we participate gives us another chance for the silent leavening of prayer. (And you did hear me say "silent," didn't you?) Moreover, as we work with people and play with them we can also pray for them. We are accepted. We are not set apart, but are part of the body of Christ. "But I thought we were supposed to be set apart!" some of you may think. Not from the body—not from the body, because that is death. Read I Cor. 12:12–31. In a sense we are set apart from the world, in that we cannot be limited by the world's standards and concepts. But we cannot be separated from the body without death. And, indeed, those prayer groups who separate themselves from the body of Christ fall into the slow death of stagnation.

On the other hand if those lay people interested in healing will take their places with humility in the midst of the congregation and will pour forth their loving prayers in every church service for the congregation, then obviously, inevitably, the love of God will abide in that church more and more and some day it will become a place full of His presence and of His healing power.

The Gift of Wisdom

"BUT IS NOT HEALING A GIFT OF THE HOLY SPIRIT?" many people ask me. Yes, it is; as common sense is a gift of the Spirit and as the illumination of the mind through visions and through prophecy is a gift of the Spirit. But this does not necessarily mean that it is a magic gift conferred only upon a few. True, some people are more gifted in healing than others are. They have a more natural faith, a livelier imagination, a stronger will and, most important of all, a closer walk with God. But just as anyone of normal intelligence can learn to read, so anyone in his own way, at his own speed, can learn to pray—or, in other words, can seek the gift of healing. We are instructed, moreover, to do this. (I Cor. 12:31.)

My own first step toward the healing ministry was precisely in desiring and asking for the gift of healing. Being moved by compassion toward someone in depression, I inquired of the minister who had helped me whether "just anyone" could try to help others in this way.

"Healing is only answered prayer," said he, after a moment of deliberation. "And anyone can learn to pray."

Therefore I prayed daily for the gift of healing—whatever that might be. No light from heaven shone upon me nor did any angel tap me on the shoulder saying, "Go and heal." I could but assume that my prayer was answered and in due time step forth by faith. True, I had from the beginning taken small, inevitable steps of faith in my own home. My baby would in times of distress lay his hands upon his small person and say "Hurt. Pray." My two older children did not make this request, not having known the experience of healing. But I formed the habit of praying for them beside their beds while they slept and though I could not prove the efficacy of this prayer of faith, often with the laying on of hands, neither in my own heart could I question it.

Finally, being moved by compassion, I went forth in faith to help a young man in critical mental illness.

And I failed. I failed miserably and, so far as I know, permanently. Why? Had I received no gift of healing? Yes, I had. For, three months later when I pulled myself together sufficiently to try again, a case of shingles was healed completely within two days.

Why, then, did I fail in such a heartbreaking way that if the Lord had not kept pushing me (I sometimes wished He would stop), I would never again have tried the prayer of faith? It was because I had not prayed another prayer which should accompany any prayer for spiritual power. I had not prayed for the very first gift of the Spirit as listed by Saint Paul (I Cor. 12:8) and as perceived in the souls of men after Pentecost: the gift of wisdom. Wisdom, according to Webster's unabridged dictionary, is "The ability to judge soundly and deal sagaciously with facts." It had not occurred to me to ask for this gift. I had taken for granted that people were wise or stupid according to the pattern of their nature and that there was nothing to be done about it. But the Bible says differently: "If any of you lack wisdom, let him ask of God, that giveth to all men liberally and upbraideth not; and it shall be given him." (James 1:5.) Now it is true that people differ in their native abilities and that a certain amount of wisdom is a native and varying gift. But it is also true, as with all gifts of the Spirit, that God can add a supernatural gift to a natural one, so that instead of "not having the sense we were born with" we can have much more sense than we were born with. We can acquire more power of clear thinking, more sagacity in dealing with facts, more direct guidance from God—all three. Guidance alone is not sufficient, for one can misunderstand the voice of God within us. I was sure that I was guided to take on the problem of the young man who was my first failure. But God needed more than merely the impulse to help. God needed more than the gift of faith, for that indeed I did have: I believed completely that the young man would be healed. God needed also wisdom: first of all the wisdom to translate God's guidance accurately. God was not saying, "Pray for him and he will be healed." God was saying, "Learn how to pray for cases like this." I needed wisdom to understand and to learn. I needed also the gift of the discernment of the spirits of men. Thank the Lord these gifts have been increased in me so that the help that I failed to give this young man I have since been able to give to many others in like circumstance.

Perhaps you are thinking in some dismay, "But how can I avoid such a failure?"

You cannot avoid every failure, any more than a soldier can avoid every difficulty. But you can surely protect yourself from so shattering a failure as mine by praying for the gift of wisdom, and also by following this hint: Do not begin with the most difficult cases.

Yes, I know all things are possible with God, but all things are not as yet possible with Agnes. The two words are not coterminous. I am grateful for all that God has done through me, but I am not as yet a wide enough channel for the full flow of the power of the Holy Spirit. No one born lame has as yet stood upon his feet and run and leaped by the mere stretching forth of my hand in the name of Jesus Christ. (Acts 3:1–9.) Therefore, one of the first works of wisdom is to decide when to stretch forth my hand and when to abstain, even as Jesus abstained when he stood by the pool of Bethesda and a great multitude of sick folk were there and He said to *one man*—and to one only—"Wilt thou be made whole?"

A young minister once said in his enthusiasm, "Any light bulb can channel any current of electricity! The light bulb does not make the electricity—electricity comes from the powerhouse and therefore is unlimited!"

An estimable young man, but he did not know much about electricity.

For many years I put on a Christmas Eve pageant. The first time I borrowed two 1000-watt floodlights, intending to place them on the floor and cover them with midnight blue gelatine. With them I meant to light my lovely angels, turning the lights on with a rheostat so that the angels would gradually appear, their blue and silver and purple and gold gleaming out from behind tall cedar trees, until their glory filled the chancel. But when I started to plug in one of the floodlights my young electrician nearly blew a fuse himself.

"What are you trying to do?" he cried. "Burn down the church?"

"Well, I want these floodlights!"

"Yes, I know. But you can't plug a thousand-watt floodlight into an ordinary outlet. It will either blow out every fuse in the church or it will start a fire."

"Then build me a larger outlet," said I. "Because I'm going to have these floodlights."

Is there no end to this building of new mansions of the soul so that we can be better ministers for God—more adequate channels for His power? No, thank God, there is not. For if we ever ceased building how dull our lives would be!

We continue praying, then, for the gift of healing—or, in other words, for the increase of the power of the Holy Spirit within us, directed toward healing. And we also continue to pray for wisdom and to try the way of wisdom as we try the way of healing: subjecting each decision to the judgment of understanding, reason and common sense. If we will pray in this way we will avoid not only the making of overambitious choices for our prayer projects but also we will avoid many other foolish moves. We will not stand on the church steps every Sunday morning as one lady told me she did, and give the minister tracts. (She did not understand why her minister still did not believe in healing!) We will not go to the pastor and tell him we have a gift of healing and offer to help him in his work, thus unconsciously identifying ourselves with the sacramental work of a trained and professional person. We will be content to help him by our silent prayers, as I have outlined before, and by going in secrecy to those whom the Lord would have us help. If we continue in this with humility the day may come when the pastor will hear of our Christian friendliness (from someone else he will hear this, not from ourselves) and perhaps ask us to go and see some troubled person. If with wisdom we put our hands upon our mouths and keep silence before him, the time may come when instead of saying, "Here's that woman again!" and ducking behind the study door he may step out to meet us with a smile of welcome.

If we are enriched with the gift of wisdom we will not go to the minister and ask him to organize a prayer group. We will know that a prayer group is an organism and not an organization, and that if we ourselves pray for those to whom the Lord leads us—and it may be someone from whom we buy a dress in a dress shop or someone who sits beside us on a bus—then the time will come when a few of us who have prayed together will spontaneously desire to meet regularly in order to uphold each other's hands in prayer. If we are wise we will not even announce this in the church bulletin lest it lose strength through publicity and lest the wrong people come out of curiosity. If church or chapel is open for prayer during the week we may unobtrusively meet there for our prayers, subject to the minister's approval. But if not, then we can meet in our own homes.

But how will the world come to know that we are doing this work if we so surround ourselves with quietness, drawing about ourselves the veil of silence? They will come gradually to know by the changed lives that they see. "By their fruits ye shall know them." And if someone asks us, saying, "What has happened to you? You are an entirely different person!" then we may tell him.

Moreover if we pray for the gift of wisdom we may know by God's grace what manner of praying people to avoid.

Yes, I do avoid some of them. I flee as from the plagues of Egypt. If a lady swoops upon me with beaming face and outstretched hands and cries, "Oh, the Lord told me to say a little prayer for you!" I step aside. For the Lord has not told me that she should elect herself as the chaplain of my soul. "Lay hands suddenly on no man," Saint Paul says (1 Tim. 5:22); and while he refers primarily I believe to ordination, nevertheless I accept the remark as divinely inspired.

If someone comes to me unsought and unheralded and says in unctuous tones, "God told me that you were to do such and such" or that such and such is going to happen to me, I cannot help questioning his "guidance." For I have learned that God is perfectly able to communicate directly with me, and if I am in doubt of the gist of His communication, then I go and check it in the mouths of two or three witnesses as the Bible says. Now it is true that there are prophets who hear the voice of God concerning me more truly than I hear it myself. But these do not lightly come to me with tales of woe or words from God, but approach with caution any warning that they are given concerning me. Tommy Tyson, a well-known Methodist evangelist, once said, "There are some people who rejoice in the afflictions of the righteous. They seem to take pleasure in prophesying evil to them. As a matter of fact, these premonitions are as apt to come from the devil as from the Lord and the telling of them can be the devil's tool, thus fastening on the person the foretold disaster. If the warnings are really from the Lord, then the one who receives the warning should himself pray for protection for his friend and should not pass on the warning lest by putting it into words he fastens it upon the person."

If we are wise we will judge righteous judgments and will decide by the fruits of prayer concerning their rightness. If a group of people pray for a troubled soul in such a way as to make him feel rejected of God—to put fear into him, to increase his trouble—then that group is led astray by the evil one and we will not identify ourselves with it. If a person who prays shakes and quivers and puffs and pants and otherwise carries on, then that one is too self-centered—is unconsciously making a play of his own prayer power—or, at best, is led astray by indiscretion and lack of control, and we may well decide to avoid such a one. If he claims that the Holy Spirit causes him to act in such disturbing ways, then let us remember the words of Scripture to the effect that the spirit of a prophet is subject to the prophet (I Cor. 14:32)—in other words, that the Holy Spirit never controls us contrary to our will: the choice is always ours. We may remind ourselves also that God is divinely courteous and would not rudely startle our friends by our surprising behavior. True, when we pray for another with the laying on of hands, a power passes through us; a real energy; an actual radiation of a kind of light that cannot usually be seen by the eyes. This may cause our hands to quiver slightly as though a current of electricity were flowing through them, which in a way it is. But we need not make a show of this, nor need we accentuate the slight quivering of the hands by concentrating upon them. If we quiet ourselves before the Lord and pray in quietness and for quietness, this tremor (which is not the actual power but is the effect of the power upon our own nerves) will become more tranquil and less conspicuous.

If we are moved to pray in the Spirit, saying words that might be incomprehensible to the other person, then we can pray thus under our breath or within the secrecy of our own minds lest our words should startle the one for whom we pray. Again you may think, "But how are they to know about the power of the Holy Spirit if we do not show forth that power?" And again I say, "By their fruits ye shall know them." By our changed lives and the changed lives of those for whom we pray the power of the Holy Spirit of Jesus Christ will become known.

The gift of wisdom, naturally, not only warns one what not to do but gives one added power and success in whatever one does. A Jewish music teacher once came to me for help in nervous and mental depression. On receiving this help and on learning how to pray the prayer of faith, he told me with delight, "I am doing it now for all my pupils! Many of them are nervous and tense and while teaching them I pray for them in my mind. And they are improving and so they are learning faster." After many years I met this man on a street in Philadelphia and he said, "I am still using the power of God in my music teaching and they have raised my salary, and they give me all the difficult pupils to help."

This man, although he did not know it, was seeking the gift of God's wisdom in his teaching; and God, who giveth to all men liberally and upbraideth not, gave him the gift even though he did not know the Holy Spirit, the Giver.

God is a Creator and therefore it was to the glory of God that one who creates ability in music should create more of this heavenly gift.

I knew a businessman who owned a fleet of trucks

and who did all to the glory of God and his business naturally grew and prospered. Moreover, since in silence he prayed for his truck drivers, they came to perceive something of this and they would call him in an emergency and say, "Mr. Jones, the wife's sick. Will you pray for her?" This man's way was the way of wisdom.

If he had become so wrapped up in religion that he desired to sell his business and devote himself to telling people about Jesus I do not think it would have been to the glory of God! He had no gift of speech. It was not in his nature to be a lecturer. But it was in his nature to be a good businessman. One hears from time to time of somone filled with zeal but not according to wisdom who neglects his work and buries his natural talents for business and expects the world to support him as he flits from place to place "testifying." If he is acting according to the gift of God's wisdom, then he will become more successful as an evangelist than he ever was as a businessman and his change of occupation will redound to the glory of God. But if this is merely self-indulgence in a pleasurable emotion of spiritual excitement, bound up perhaps with a bit of self-seeking and a modicum of laziness, it will not redound to the glory of God.

"Whatsoever ye do, do all to the glory of God."

And never forget that God is a maker, a doer, a worker—a Creator! His creativity moreover functions on every plane, not merely on that plane that we are pleased to call "spiritual." If there were no bridge-builders in the world and no automobile mechanics, no schoolteachers and no inventors, the world that God is building through man upon this planet would fall to pieces. If, on the other hand, we would all seek God's gift of wisdom in whatever we do, we would create with an efficiency, an integrity, a vision, greater than anything we have yet seen, and God's Kingdom of Heaven would have a material framework in which to grow.

The gift of wisdom and the gift of knowledge, to be discussed in a later chapter, are not two separate gifts tied up in different packages, but are closely related aspects of the general working of the Holy Spirit, which is to edify and to endue with power. The Holy Spirit will guide us as to those things that it is good for us to know and will help us to understand and to know them. The Holy Spirit, however, acts always in accordance with the laws of our own natures, which are not identical, and never against them. If He gives us, for instance, the urge to write books, then that gift of writing is within us even though it may not as yet have been released. But if we think that because someone else has written a book therefore we can write a book if only we have enough paper and pencils and can find the time, then we are in error and the book, fortunately, will never be written.

In other words, God gives the gift of wisdom to all men liberally but not equally. Saint Paul has made this quite clear in the twelfth chapter of First Corinthians. There, he compares us to different parts in the body of Christ and points out that if we were all the same, with equal gifts, there could be no body.

Man is always trying to standardize. God, with a ruthless hand, destroys the pattern of standardization from time to time because it is going contrary to the very principle of creativity that He has wrought into the world. Let us therefore seek the gift of wisdom not that we shall be like someone else, not that we shall forsake our work and seek something more "spiritual" —but that we shall do a better job in whatever our kind of work is, according to our temperament, our natural gifts, and our opportunities.

5

The Way of Love

Now suppose we have tried to meditate upon and
to carry out all that is said in the previous chapters
and still find little power in our prayers. Are we then
without hope? No! Not while we live or while the
Lord lives! Then what is the block?

It may be that we are not sufficiently enwrapped in
the mantle of love. We have prayed for the gift of
healing and for the gift of wisdom. Perhaps we have
read the twelfth chapter of First Corinthians and have
prayed for other more mysterious gifts. But have we
considered the last verse of this same chapter: "And
yet shew I unto you a more excellent way." Or as Prof.
J. B. Phillips says in his modern translation, "I shall
show you what is the highest way of all." Or again as
another modern student of the Bible has translated,
"Behold I point out to you an incomparable way."
What does this mean? That the gift of love is the

highest gift? Not at all. Saint Paul does not call love a gift, he calls it a *way*. A way for what and toward what? A way of life! A way of using all the gifts of the Spirit! We might read chapter thirteen as follows, changing its form so that its meaning may impress us more clearly: "If I speak with the tongues of men and angels *and have charity*, I am not as sounding brass or as a tinkling cymbal. And if I have the gift of prophecy . . . and have all faith so that I can remove mountains *and have charity*, I am something! And if I bestow all my goods to feed the poor and give my body to be burned *and have charity*, it profiteth me greatly." This last verse used to puzzle me until I translated it like this: "And though I give my money and my life to worthy causes and get myself persecuted in order to prove something—and do it not out of love but out of anger—it profiteth me nothing." Or again I might say, if I teach healing to show others how wrong they are or to attain advantage to myself, materially or spiritually, it profiteth me nothing. The Bible does not say that doing good for inadequate motives profits nobody! It may still accomplish worthy ends. But it profits *us* nothing; it does not take away the darkness of our minds or the dullness of our souls or the illness of our bodies.

Saint Paul is not expounding love as another gift, but as the over-all enveloping bloodstream of God, permeating all the gifts. The specialized gifts of the Spirit—healing, faith, discernment and so forth—are our tool kit, to quote the Rev. Dr. Francis Whiting, Director of Evangelism in the Baptist Church of Michigan. They are the tools with which we do the work of God. To say, "I will not use these tools; I will just draw my pay check" would not be sensible. How can we have the pay check if we have not done the work? How can we have the fruits of the Spirit—love, joy, and peace—if we have failed to obey the Spirit? The Holy Spirit through Jesus Christ our Captain commands us to go forth and seek and save those who are lost. (Mark 16:15–19.) In order to do this adequately, we need gifts of faith, of healing and of miracles. Love is the beginning and the ending of all our work and the enfolding mantle in which all the gifts of the Spirit are cherished and protected.

This love is not merely a gift, it is a whole way of life. We can not receive it in full unless we give it forth to others, especially to those who have injured us. "Forgive us our trespasses as we forgive those who trespass against us." This is the only petition (or affirmation) in the Lord's Prayer that is conditional. Why? Because of our nature, because of the way we are made. The mind and the body so interrelate that unforgiveness acts as a poison within us, and this is so no matter how worthy the cause over which we fret and fume. The bodily results of fury are quite evident: we lose our appetite, we can neither eat nor digest, the nerves tighten in spine and head, the mind is confused, the knees shake; the whole body is out of line with life, which is love because God is love. The effects of our usual feelings of a dull resentment and an old bitterness are even more devastating because they are not so obvious, but they eat upon the body like a slow poison. We express this in our common speech: "Something's eating on him"; "It gives me a pain in the neck"; "I can't stomach it"; "You make me sick," and so forth.

There is a wonderful picture of this slow death in Dr. Rebecca Beard's book, *Everyman's Search*. Also this is pointed up most dramatically in *Arthritis, Medicine, and the Spiritual Laws* by Dr. Loring T. Swaim, a specialist in arthritis who found that he could not heal the body unless he could help the patient heal the poisoning resentments in his subconscious, or, as the Bible would say, the "heart."

But let us not despair, for we can be set free from this slow poison. There is a quick and miraculous way of being set free and there is a slow but equally sure (and possibly more lasting) way.

The quick way is an instantaneous and overwhelming experience of the love of Christ, a conversion or reconversion experience which comes to people usually through the prayer of another. When in England last summer I met a young man who had been troubled both with arthritis and with epilepsy. Also since childhood he had felt a bitter hate toward a woman who had broken up his home. I quote from his own story of his conversion, taken from the parish magazine of the Anglican church through whose ministry he found Christ:

"What of the miracles? The greatest miracle that has been worked on me was my being 'born again,' my becoming a spiritual being, born into God's Family. Since then the Lord has cured me of epilepsy, a

disease that would have prevented me being used by
God, for I could not remember things, neither could I
concentrate on studying anything. But for the past two
years since I was 'born again' I have never felt like
having another attack, also I have never been as
physically fit in all my life as I have during the past
two years."

In his own story told to me he added the fact that
his arthritis had disappeared as well as his epilepsy,
and indeed to this I can testify, having seen this
radiant and stalwart young man. He also told me a
most significant fact: that as the love of Christ poured
through him, his hatred toward the woman who had
wrecked his home simply melted away.

Would that every minister of every church, instead
of using his confirmation classes to teach the Prayer
Book and the Church Seasons or to air his personal
views on social problems of the day, would lead his
people to Jesus, that He can teach them what He wills
by filling them with His love so that they are born
again!

Let me quote from a sermon preached by the rector
of this same Anglican church, the Reverend Patrick
Ashe.

"One day a lady came to see me. She told me about
some relations who had been beastly to her. She was
angry and hurt; there was no one she could talk to
about it, as it was a family row, so she bottled it up.

"At first she used to lie awake at night thinking out
what she might have said—or what she would say. She
had endless conversations in her head, that went on

into the early hours of the morning, till she fell asleep exhausted. In time the imaginary conversations got less, but she still found she could not get to sleep.

"She also found that whenever she thought about the woman who had hurt her, she began to breathe more heavily, and her hand trembled. If she met the woman in the street she felt like jelly. As time went on, even when she was not actually thinking about her, she got out of breath. She went to the doctor, who was not quite sure what was the matter with her. But he gave her pills to help her sleep, and a spray to help her breathing.

"One day in Church the lesson was from Saint Matthew's Gospel, chapter 6, when Jesus taught His disciples the Lord's Prayer. She knew the Lord's Prayer, of course, and often said it. But it never registered very much. She often got to the end without actually thinking about what she had said.

"But that day she heard the next two verses [Matt. 6:14–15]: 'For if ye forgive men their trespasses, your heavenly Father will also forgive you: but if ye forgive not men their trespasses, neither will your Father forgive your trespasses.' That day it registered. She had been saying, 'Forgive us our trespasses as we forgive them who have trespassed against us.' . . . What about the other woman? She had never forgiven her. That day she knew she must forgive her. She also knew that she could not.

"What was she to do? She felt so bitter and angry and resentful, it was making her ill. She knew that. She knew she must forgive at all costs. But she just could not.

"I reminded her what Jesus had said when he was on the Cross about the people who were killing him. He said, 'Father forgive them.'

"I asked her: Jesus was a hundred per cent without blame—was she absolutely one hundred per cent blameless?

"No, she said, not quite one hundred per cent.

"Was what the other woman had done to her as bad as having nails hammered into her hands and feet, and being left to gasp to death in agony on a cross in the blazing sun?

"She spoke decisively: No, definitely not—in comparison, what she had suffered was very little.

"But Jesus forgave, and He has offered to come and live in our hearts. If she asked Him into her heart, she would be *able* to forgive. This was His promise. It was God's offer. She could receive that sort of nature, loving and forgiving, the spirit that was in Jesus.

"So we knelt, and she prayed simply and sincerely. She said, 'I'm sorry, Lord Jesus, for my resentment and for many other sins. Thank you for your forgiveness. Please come into my heart and fill me with your Spirit of love.'

"Some weeks later she came glowing. The hard lump of resentment had melted. She had prayed for her relative. She had gone to see her and said she was sorry for her part in the quarrel. There had been a reconciliation.

"She no longer needed sleeping pills and she looked ten years younger.

"Jesus said, 'Without me ye can do nothing.' Paul

said, 'I can do all things through Christ which strengtheneth me.'

" 'Forgive us . . . as we forgive' we can't, unless and until Jesus is dwelling in our hearts."

This woman was already a committed Christian, but she had not realized the connection between forgiveness and health. When she did realize it, the rector led her to the forgiveness of Christ in such a direct and heart-touching way that she, too, had a spiritual experience in answer to a direct prayer for forgiveness and for the Holy Spirit.

Yes. It is possible to attain immediately to a state of forgiveness. And what chains drop away from the soul as we do so!

However, for your comfort let me say that there is also the slow way of learning to live in love. I myself did not burst into any sudden freedom. I had to overcome my old dull resentments little by little, one by one. At this point I could bring in words such as "surrender" and "commitment" and "consecration." The words would be, in their meaning, accurate. One is surrendered. One is committed. Therefore, whether one likes it or not, one is consecrated. But I shall not use these words because I don't like them. Their emotional context is to me false. They suggest tears of repentance and "I give my heart to You" prayers. They suggest a joyous and triumphant marching up an aisle, a falling upon one's knees and saying to the delighted congregation, "I surrender my life to Jesus." They suggest hugging to one's bosom a holy love, so that one's total being is consecrated to Christ. I do not scorn these words. I have often longed to be able to feel them. When I draw away from people who use these words, it is not because I despise them! It is because, out of a lonely heart, I envy them. For the greater part of my life I have been utterly unable to feel any love toward Christ at all. Yes, I know I tell people He loves them. He does. I know it. Yes, people tell me often that they feel great floods of love through me. Well, praise the Lord. But I do not feel anything. Why? Because for too many years the doors of my unconscious were closed to the feeling of love. Then why have I done the things I have done? Why have I denied the desires of my own heart: painting and gardening and all the quiet and lovely activities that delight me, and instead traveled over the cold world telling people of God's power to heal? Why? Well, why would you run into a burning house to bring out someone who is in danger? Why would you leap into deep water to save a drowning man? You just do it, that's all. You do not stop to analyze your feelings. You do it because there is a need. It is the misfortune of some of us that when we were very young the doors of the unconscious closed to the sensation of love: to put it in other words, one built too strong a barrier to feeling, lest one be hurt overmuch. It does not take very terrible wounds to close a sensitive soul to the life-giving feeling of love. Some day in God's mercy He may find a way to open those doors for you as He has done for me, and the way will be told in another chapter. But now I want to point out this: feeling or no feeling, one can *act* love. And the acting of love is honored and blessed—perhaps all the more so in that it is done simply from obedience and out of a concern for people, not on the drive of an emotion.

So to you who cannot feel the love of Christ like a warm current of life within your heart, let me say, *you have that love whether you feel it or not.* He loves you even if at the moment you are not aware of the liberating joy of His love. Furthermore, you love Him and He knows it. If you cannot feel it and only love Him in action by doing what He tells you to do—seeking and saving those who are lost in darkness of mind or illness of body—then He knows it all the more surely and is grateful for it. And if the Bible is true at all, He will reward you, not only in heaven but in this life as well. (Mark 10:29–30.) So be comforted. He will not leave you comfortless, but He will come to you.

Moreover, you can prepare for Him a highway, that He may come more quickly. You can clear that highway by removing the rocks of resentment toward others that tend to accumulate over the years. And this you do by an act of forgiveness.

I have already described a way of forgiveness, using the creative imagination. In this book I have recounted it as one of the exercises of prayer that we do in church for the healing of the congregation: the body of Christ. In all my books this way of life is explained and illustrated. I now add to these oft-given expositions a special suggestion for those who cannot *feel* love. First of all, since our feelings have grown so dull, we may fail to recognize within us hate or resentment. We can find it, however, if we look into ourselves with the searchlight of truth. So I suggest that you look for any lack of loving-kindness within you by asking yourself, "Whom can I learn to like better?" That is an inescapable question in its simplicity and its directness. (I might add that if you really believe there is no person or race or nation whom you could possibly like any better than you already do, you need to consult a psychiatrist.)

Having found someone toward whom you should feel more kindly, I suggest a way of changing one's relationship by action. "Put on therefore . . . holy and beloved, bowels of mercies (Col. 3:12), or as the Revised Version more delicately puts it, "a heart of compassion." *Do* something, not only to show kindness to the other person but, more importantly, to indicate to your own subconscious that it is your will to love.

The wife of a retired minister was once grievously hurt and enraged because the new minister asked everyone else of any significance to walk in the procession at the next confirmation service, but did not ask her husband. (Probably the poor young minister simply forgot to do so. It is very easy to forget the obvious.) She was under strong temptation to sally forth into the congregation and make an unholy row. (Any female of the species is able to do this when roused.) Though she did not embark upon this venture, her demeanor as she sailed out of church left no doubt about her feelings.

However, she realized on reaching home that if she allowed herself to remain in this state of anger it would do her no good either physically or spiritually and it would weaken her power to help others. Therefore she had to remove this feeling from her mind, like it or not. So she bought a present for the newest baby and the next afternoon simply made a call, congratulating the minister and his wife and giving the baby a pink sweater. What fun to see the relief on the minister's face—the relaxed warmth with which a cup of coffee was offered and cookies were shared—the deep comfort of going home again in friendship and not in wrath!

"But wouldn't it have been better to talk the whole thing out with the minister?" some of you may wonder. It might have been easier. But not, I think, better.

There are times when "talking it out" accomplishes peace. But there are other times when talking it out only makes matters worse. Only the one who is in a position to apologize can resolve a situation by talking it out, for the words that make peace are the words "I'm sorry." If the minister had been the one seeking forgiveness, he could have found it in this manner. But for the woman to go to the minister and explain to him what she thought of him would in all likelihood only have made more trouble—especially by the time the congregation was regaled with stories of the classic fight between minister and lady.

There is a difference between false kindness and true kindness. To wear at all times a mask of pleasantness in order to hide our real feelings is not good, for we tend to go our way and forget what manner of person we really are, as the Bible says. (James 1:24.) In other words, if we repress our feelings beneath a false courtesy too long and too continuously we tend to deny their reality. Then, as we all know, they can brood within our subconscious minds and bring forth fruit of depression and bitterness. Especially in the relationship of marriage and family life, we should love each other enough to dare to share in love not only our joys but also our sorrows, not only our pleasure in each other but also the wounded feelings that from time to time we feel. It is the privilege of love so to share that our understanding may be deepened and that we may mend our ways together.

But without the intention of forgiveness, the mere unbridling of the tongue and uttering of harsh words is not in the long run therapeutic or desirable. It is sad to see certain church groups today attempt to heal the soul by stirring up hate. Momentarily it may give a person release to bite and devour someone else—to speak forth his hidden grievances and give voice to his hates. (Gal. 5:15.) But merely giving voice to these feelings does not necessarily remove them. It may for a moment refresh a person to permit his worst self a bit of a romp. But unless it is followed by forgiveness and love, those harsh words will rebound upon him again and to his original feelings of hate there will be added more hate because he has to justify himself in a behavior of which he is becoming ashamed. In other words, his conscience will very likely call to mind certain verses of Scripture: "Whosoever shall say to his brother, 'Raca,' shall be in danger of the council;

but whosoever shall say, 'Thou fool,' shall be in danger of hell fire." (Matt. 5:22.) The One who said these words was the greatest psychologist the world has seen, being not only a student of the mind of man but also the Creator of the mind of man. He has given to us the greatest tool of power ever given to man: the tool of forgiveness, which is the stirring up of divine love. That Christian people should deliberately teach the stirring up of anger instead of love is a shocking thing! I heard of a Training Group that as usual sat about a table waiting for an explosion of hitherto suppressed anger to "release" them. There was a long silence. Finally one of the brethren said, "Let us pray." His suggestion was met with anger. They did not want to pray. They were courting the devil, not the Lord. Perhaps they did not know that there is a devil. This might account for their carelessness in opening doors to him.

But how could they know the hidden evil of their hearts if they did not incite each other to spew forth angry words? They could have known by asking the Holy Spirit to show them their own hidden sins and then by listening. And being convicted by the voice of God they could then have sought forgiveness for themselves and given forgiveness to others. So shall we some day have a Kingdom of Heaven on earth—so and in no other way. For unless we forgive those who trespass against us we are closing ourselves to the forgiveness of God and without that there is no redemption.

I used to say in the Presbyterian church, "Forgive us

our debts as we forgive our debtors." Doubtless both meanings are implicit in the original words of the Lord's Prayer. My friend Mary Welch said strong words about the reality of this commandment. A minister came to her afterwards and told her that for a long time someone had owed him three hundred dollars. "I need that money," he said. "And he doesn't need it. Yet I've asked him for it time and again and he has not sent it to me. Do you really mean that I should forgive that debt?"

"That is what Jesus said," replied Mary.

"Well, what should I do? Write and tell him that he need not pay it?"

"Oh, no. The paying of the debt is his responsibility. But the overcoming of resentment is your responsibility. Just forgive him in your heart, so that whether he ever pays the debt or not, you feel only kindness toward him."

"I don't know that I can," hesitated the minister.

"Probably you can't, all by yourself. But if we ask Jesus to help you, then you can—or He can within you."

So they prayed together, and together they sent the words of forgiveness toward the man at a distance. Two days later the minister came and showed her a letter from the man containing a check for three hundred dollars! "Does forgiveness always do that?" he wondered.

"Forgiveness always opens doors," said Mary. "It always removed barriers. Often, though not always, the very thing that was denied to our wrath comes freely forth to us."

"But forgiveness such as this is difficult!" you are thinking. Yes. True forgiveness requires a man of strength, a woman of courage. Any undisciplined man can bluster and shout. Any weakling of a woman can whine and cry. It takes courage even to hide the emotions and to discipline the tongue. But to *change* the emotions, converting hate into love, bitterness into tenderness, resentment into compassion—this requires the full strength of a Son of God! It is the most difficult venture in the whole world, this ordering and training of the soul in forgiveness. But it is the training required of us for the life of the Spirit. Our indulgences in anger and frustration and irritation have weakened the whole Christian church, just as football players who indulge themselves by lolling in bed instead of practising weaken the whole team.

Conversely, it is in forgiving our personal injuries that we learn to pass on to strangers—to the downtrodden and the lost—the forgiveness of Christ.

I could tell a hundred stories of this most quiet and yet most noble Christian work, but I will choose only one.

There lives in the deep South a little old lady who, being filled with the Spirit, goes forth to seek and to save those who are most truly lost. She is known in prisons and in poorhouses and in dives and in joints. She heard one day of a murderer—a multiple and confessed murderer—who was condemned to die. She went to see him. She knew that she could not save his life, forfeited to the laws of the land. But she could bring him out of that death of the soul which he had already suffered.

"You can't go in there, Miss Nellie!" said the guard. "He's dangerous. We never go into his cell alone—it takes two or three of us to manage him."

"He won't bother me," said Miss Nellie serenely.

"But alone ——"

"I'm not alone," said Miss Nellie. And the guard, knowing what she meant, stepped aside and let her into the cell.

The great black man leaped from his bed, cursing and swearing and shouting.

Miss Nellie merely stood still and prayed for him, seeing with the eyes of Christ the real man behind the savage—the real man simple, childlike, capable of a great love and a real holiness. Because she could see the real man and because she poured out upon him the Holy Spirit of Christ—or, in other words, the love of God in action—he ceased raving after a while, at least long enough to draw breath.

"I understand," murmured the mother of many children and grandchildren. "I'm real sorry you have to go to State Penitentiary. . . ." By which she meant, and he knew that she meant, to the electric chair.

"You don't understand!" roared the captive. "Nobody ever done understand me! My mother didn't and my father didn't and ——"

"Jesus understands you," said Miss Nellie.

Whereupon the tormented man began once more to shout curses, shaking his huge clenched hands at the ceiling. "Don't give me none of that Jesus crap!" he yelled.

Not in the least intimidated, Miss Nellie simply stood there and prayed for him. Whether at this moment she was aware of feeling love for him I do not know, but I doubt it. My guess would be that she was, in her spirit, too truly *him* to feel anything *for* him in the conscious mind. This deep identification through the Spirit goes far beyond any detectable emotion. She was him and yet she was also herself praying for him, as an actor on the stage is the person whom he portrays and at the same time also himself interpreting that person to the audience.

After a while there was a brief silence. Then he cried out to her, "What's dat? What dat I feels? What's a-comin' all over me?"

"That is the Holy Spirit," said Miss Nellie serenely.

"But I'm happy! I never felt like dis in my whole life!"

"That's the joy of the Lord," Miss Nellie explained.

For an hour or more she sat on the crude pallet beside this man and told him very simply the story of the love of Jesus and of the Holy Spirit of Jesus, while tears ran down his cheeks and shouts of joy rang from time to time out into the corridors to the amazement of the guards and the other prisoners.

The next week she went again to see him. Before she reached the jail she caught sight of him looking out from behind the bars, his hands flung high in the air in praise. "He ain't left me yet!" he shouted to her. "He ain't left me yet!"

Before this man went to the electric chair he converted every prisoner on his corridor. The last man he converted was the executioner. For he walked to the electric chair in the glory of God as a man about to enter into heaven, which indeed he was.

"I'll never do it again," said the executioner. "I can't."

But is this a story of forgiveness? Yes, in the highest sense it is. It is not personal forgiveness, it is a greater forgiveness—the giving of the love of Christ through the Holy Spirit, who is God in action.

Do you begin to see in this a key to power and a key to love and a key to the opening of doors into the Kingdom of Heaven? Then praise the Lord! "For the earnest expectation of the creature waiteth for the manifestation of the sons of God." (Rom. 8:19.)

6

The Gift of Knowledge

SUPPOSING NOW THAT WE HAVE FOLLOWED TO THE FULL
the suggestions given in these chapters: we have
opened our lives to God's creation and to His creativity, we have learned the prayer of faith and we have
forgiven those who have hurt us. Are we then perfect?
If so, whence arise the times of an inner dullness?
Why does heaviness tend to creep over us so that we
wake of a morning listless and out of sorts? Is it simply
that we need more faith and more forgiveness and
more creativity? Possibly so, but something blocks us
from receiving. Is it that we need another experience
of holy joy manifested in the gift of tongues, or of
"ecstatic utterance," as someone has called it? Many
people suggest this as the remedy for all ills, but I do
not agree that the same medicine cures everything. I
have seen people in a dangerous mental condition
because instead of dealing with the trouble of the

deep mind they merely sought more surface stimulation from the Spirit.

Something is troubling the deep mind. There is no question about it. Some old unpleasant memory is knocking on the doors of the consciousness. Some need of the soul is arising as a dark shadow that will overwhelm us if we do not let it out into the light of understanding. We do indeed need more of the Holy Spirit at times such as these, but the gift we need is the gift of knowledge, particularly the knowledge and understanding of our own souls. And it is the primary work of the Holy Spirit to give us this understanding if we will but ask and listen to His answer.

What are these "roots of bitterness" and how can they be drawn out of us? In other words, what are the causes of our present low periods, with their ungovernable wanderings of distressful thoughts? Even though these sorrows are bound up with present circumstances, yet they have their roots in the past. A thought pattern of sorrow has been built in the past and the emotional reactions of the present follow it as one's wandering footsteps tend to follow a path through the meadows. Fortunately there are many good and lovely thought patterns also among the memories: the delicious excitement of Christmas Eve, with its mysterious packages and its lighted Christmas trees and the luminous radiance of the Baby in the manger somehow wistfully shining through it all; the first peach blossoms in the spring, shaking out a breathtaking curtain of rosy delight over the brown fields; birds in the high sky singing and flying. . . .

All these are open windows to the joy of the eternal country from whence we came. These memories we cherish, and happy are those who have many of them. But among these hoarded bits of beauty there are memories of ugliness and of hurt. We try to forget them but we cannot. If they come up into the conscious mind we push them down again, saying, "No, I mustn't think of that." We would be wise to turn away from them if they could not be transformed into beautiful memories, for why should we spend our adult life brooding over what we cannot help? But it is a mistake to turn away, for they *can* be transformed.

Another mistake that we sometimes make is to assume that this pursuing shadow, this devious impulse, this besetting fear, is necessarily "the devil," and to cast it out instead of wrestling with it until it will give us its name. In other books I have warned of the danger of mistaking the voice of the devil for the voice of God: saying some dishonorable or unkind thing for instance and adding, "God told me to say this." It is equally possible to mistake the voice of God for the voice of the devil. The Holy Spirit comes into the world not merely to make us comfortable but also to make us uncomfortable: to convict us: to show us our hidden sins and our forgotten sorrows so that we can find ways of healing them.

Therefore I believe that our next step is to look within ourselves and say to the Lord, "What is it?" and listen. (Those of us forced into prayer through mental depression could not have done this in the beginning. But now we can.)

Some of us have been taught that "salvation" is accomplished automatically once we have accepted Jesus Christ. Others have been persuaded that the Holy Spirit Himself takes away all our fears and temptations without our needing to concern ourselves with the matter.

Sometimes, indeed, He does, thank God! We change inwardly and do not even know that we have changed. For example, I was brought up with a well-founded fear of dogs. My parents were pioneer missionaries in an inland city of China, where the "wonks" snarled at our heels with bared fangs and with every expectation of biting us. When I migrated alone to the United States at the age of fifteen the fear came with me. Once I spent some weeks helping an aunt who did missionary work in the mountains of Virginia. One day I walked down the road and two huge animals about the size of small horses shot off the front porch of a rickety cabin and down the hillside after me, death and destruction in their frothing jaws.

"Don't be skeered!" shrilled the mountain woman encouragingly from her doorway. "They don't often bite womenfolks!"

But I was scared.

However, after some years my mother, returned on furlough, remarked to me, "Why, Agnes! When did you stop being afraid of dogs?"

And I replied, genuinely surprised, "I don't know. Was I ever afraid of dogs?"

What method had God used to heal me of this fear? I would not be surprised if He had used His servants the dogs! For after I began to live in the light of God, every dog would draw near to me in spite of my uneasy shrinking and indicate in some fashion that he approved of me.

How many roots of fear and bitterness have been pulled out of us without our knowing when or why, we cannot say. But there nevertheless remain in many people other hurtful memories that God does not remove save with the co-operation of the conscious mind. For one reason or another there is something we should *do* about these matters and it would be to our hurt rather than to the good of our souls if we were automatically healed of them.

We need to understand, in order that we may learn. Sometimes, as in the following story, it is very easy to attain to this understanding if we are only willing.

Once, in years past, I found myself running the Women's Auxiliary. The manner of it was thus: I prayed during an interim between presidents, "O Lord, please put it into the mind of one of these ladies to be president."

The Lord replied in the startling way in which He sometimes does speak, "Do it yourself."

"Oh, no, Lord!" I protested. "That wasn't my idea at all!"

But the inner voice persisted: "Do it yourself."

So I let it be known through the grapevine that if sufficiently urged I would consider being president of the Women's Auxiliary, and being quite desperate, they did urge me and with becoming modesty I accepted.

Having accepted, I used the power of prayer and of faith and became a good president. (The gift of faith can be used not only for the healing of soul or body but also for the financial affairs of this world.)

But the effort took its toll in nervous tension. On a certain occasion, after we had given a bridge party to earn money for the heathen, I backed the car furiously out of the drive and into a Bell Telephone Company truck on the other side of the street.

You know the awful scrunch when metal meets metal. I climbed out of the car and looked. "That's not a very big dent in the fender," I said to myself.

But I could not quite believe it. I tried another approach: "If God wanted me to tell about this," said I to myself looking hopefully up and down the street, "I'm sure He could see to it that the driver appeared, and I don't see the driver anywhere."

I could not quite make myself believe that, either.

But now I thought up a really good one. "I am insured," I thought. "And no doubt the truck is also insured. I don't understand about insurance, but I know it takes care of everything, so I have nothing to bother about."

I decided to forget the truck.

After a while my spirits flagged. I became irritable, dull, listless. But when the matter of the truck came up into my mind I would push it down again. "No! Get down there," I would say.

I had an appointment to see an ill child and I became less and less inclined to see her. As the time drew near I found myself thinking, "Oh, I *can't!*" And if I had put the reasons for this hesitation into words they would have been "I am not worthy." (How often do people say, "I am not worthy!" But I do not think the Lord accepts that as an excuse. I think the Lord expects them to *get* worthy.) So I telephoned the little girl. "I'm off the beam somehow today and if I do come I know nothing will happen," I said. "Let's wait a day or so till I feel better and then make another date."

In the morning I awoke with a headache. "What is it, Lord?" I asked.

And the Lord said, "It's that telephone truck."

I called up the telephone company and related the incident, wrote a check for three dollars for repairing the damage—which would otherwise have been taken from the driver's pay—and immediately the joy and the power and the wholeness of the Lord returned to me.

And the headache went away. The message had got through, so there was no longer any need for the subconscious mind to give me a headache. I have spoken of the voice of the Lord remarking "It's that telephone truck" and I have spoken of the subconscious mind giving me the message. Both are true. I do not mean by "the voice of the Lord" the voice that shook the heavens, that thundered across the aeons and out of time. I mean only the still, small voice that speaks within our deep minds. The actual words may not have been His. But the comprehension of the nature of my trouble was brought up by Him out of the unconscious and was clothed in those words.

But what if I had not said, "Lord, what's the matter," on awaking? In a few more days I would have succeeded in burying that truck so deep within my memories that it could have been totally repressed. And there would have been one more unhealed memory in the junk heap at the bottom of my subconscious mind.

How many telephone trucks do you have on your junk heap?

And what if they are so far back in the years and are buried so deep that you have completely forgotten them—or you have so rationalized and explained them away that you are totally self-deceived concerning them? We all know the person who says, "Oh, yes indeed. I do love my sister-in-law and I treat her with all Christian charity—in fact I give her the best of everything in the house—but, my dear, if you *knew* what she says about *me!*" Hate and resentment bristles in the air around her and she has deceived nobody in all the world except her own conscious mind.

I have said: ask of the Lord and listen. I might say also: obey. If the voice of the Lord says, "You really hate your sister-in-law," then believe that voice and set about forgiving her! For no amount of arguing will still that little voice, and if the hate is again repressed it will fester in the deep mind and do more harm than ever. If the Lord says, "You have been dishonest," then believe Him and obey, making reparation if it is possible to do so.

Sometimes, however, even though we listen, even though we obey, we feel that there is something else blocking our joy and our power and we do not know what it is. It may be so far back in our memories that the conscious mind cannot grasp it in words.

Well, then, God can speak to us in other ways. Sometimes He shows us truths about ourselves in dreams. With the dream He often gives us the interpretation thereof, even as He did to His servant Joseph long ago: in other words, if we hold the dream up before Him and ask Him what it means He can help us to understand its message. It will assist us to understand dreams if we know that dreams are usually subjective and almost always symbolic. God is not so apt to tell us something of the world as to tell us something of ourselves. The people we dream about are apt to symbolize some part of our own nature. If I were to dream that my sister was sick I would know that some part of my feminine being—the "feeling" part of me—was in need of attention or consideration. This might be guidance to cease from too constant work and rest my woman's soul by doing some gardening or making jelly. . . . If I were to dream that I was trying to climb a very steep mountain with the help of a man and found myself slipping, I would take it to mean that my more masculine aspect—the writer or lecturer—was slipping in some area and I would try to find that area and consider the nature of its trouble.

There are times, however, when the meaning of the dream eludes me entirely, because the trouble has nothing to do with my present life or relationships. We are apt to drag chains fastened upon our souls so long ago that we do not even know what they are.

What can we do about the chains of time—the burdens put upon our souls when we were too little to be responsible? If the sorrows of a child can weigh still upon the soul of a grown person and if the fears of a child transfer themselves into irrational phobias in the mind of a grown person, then what hope is there for anyone, our personalities being so intricately involved with time and Time?

Yet there is hope, because God Himself is intricately involved with time and Time, and because, seeing our need, He incarnated Himself and became man, thus entering into the collective unconscious of the race: into the deep mind of every person; there being available for healing and for help. And He has provided not only one way but many ways of giving this help.

I have mentioned the primary step that we need to take and that we can take alone: the step of self-examination. This is not recommended to the faltering mind of a serious depressive, but is most definitely required of us as soon as we learn to walk according to His laws.

However, thank the Lord we do not always have to walk alone, for there are times when we need each other; a friend or counselor may grasp the message of the subconscious mind when the conscious mind is too harassed or too confused to understand it. Some people have a wise counselor who can help them in interpreting dreams and in self-understanding. However, being of an independent turn of mind I am rather glad that in my days of deep depression I knew nothing of psychiatry or psychology and had no professional counselor at all. God sent me friends in prayer, sometimes one, sometimes another, and often the word of a friend illumined some corner of my mind and pointed the way to the solution of a problem. A discerning young woman once said to me, "As I was praying it came to me that there is a fear in you which is connected with the eighth year of your life."

This struck me as authentic. If she had said, "God told me you were to go and see So-and-So and pray for her," I am afraid I would have suspected a slight unconscious tendency to influence my will by her will.

But I tested the guidance, harkened to the words of my friend and said, "What is it, Lord?"

Then I sent my mind back in time and tried to remember the eighth year of my life and to review it, so that God through the subconscious mind could put His finger on a sore spot and say "That is it." It was an outstanding year, for it was spent in our summer home, Kuling, due to my father's failing health. It was a year full of happy memories—white violets, lace-leaved, blooming in dark loam; mountaintops red and purple with wild azaleas; the Big Stream foaming down the valley overhung with a more fragrant foam of blossoming shrubs all growing wild in a wonderland of beauty. Yet, as I searched, I remembered among these lovely pictures another picture that was filled with fear: I saw myself standing at the window, nose to pane, watching for my father and mother to come home from their afternoon walk and being literally sick with terror. I remembered also that never in my life had I spoken of this fear to anyone. And God brought me to see, what I had never seen before, that I had hidden the cause of the fear even from myself. For the first time, following the hint given by a friend, I realized that I had feared that my father would die.

Now of what use could this be, this remembering of the cause? Would it relieve my fear merely to understand it and say to myself, "So I must learn to live with it?"

I do not think so. "But I don't want to learn to live with it!" my rebellious soul shouted within me, knowing that there is a better way than this. I went back in the memories and found that little child, and, playing a game in the imagination, I told her that she was loved and comforted and that she would also be healed. Opening thus a door into the past, I took Jesus with me and led Him to her that He might heal her with His love. And being of a sacramental church, I went to Communion service the next Sunday taking her with me.

When I turned back and found that little child in me and took her to Jesus in the way that was most natural to me, then the door was opened so that Jesus Christ entered into that living memory and healed it just as though He had walked back through time and found the little girl and had taken the fear away from her by restoring to her a father whole and joyous and able to show his love. I do not say that this was completely or instantaneously done, but I do say that perceiving the beginning of a certain fear and believing that Jesus Christ could take that fear away began a healing.

A friend helped me to look back. Now let me help you to look back, you who read this. Remember. Do not be afraid to remember, for Our Lord, already within you, will come into that memory if you ask Him to do so. (He does not enter without invitation, for He respects your own individuality and abides by your own will.) Remember, then, and imagine Him walking back with you through time and finding the small person who was agonized and torn apart—by the mother's sorrows and the father's, by rejection or homelessness or the loss of father or mother. How can He come into that memory and change it? I do not know. It is the greatest of all mysteries. But I know that He *can* do so.

This is difficult. Yes, I know. And do not blame yourself if you cannot believe the words even as you say them. Do not beat your breast and think, "I have no faith." Your conscious mind believes them; in other words, it is your will to believe them. But the wound of the old memories is deep and the defensive shell that the subconscious mind has built around them is hard. Your own words have not been able to crack it open. The deep mind is too familiar with your words. "Oh, it's only you talking again," says the little mind within and abides skulking within his self-built cage.

So let us find a way of convincing that little mind. First, I shall write out in a general way the prayer that I would pray in a more particular way if I were with you. Read this over once in silence and then find a

·time when you can be alone and uninterrupted and read it aloud. As you read, pretend that you are not hearing the words from your own lips, but from mine—not mine as a human being, but mine as a spiritual being whose spiritual body God can use as a trained channel for the healing of the soul. And know that if you take the trouble to read this aloud, in some mysterious way God *will* use me thus, and He will accomplish that which He so longs to accomplish for you and in you.

I shall now remind us both that Jesus Christ is with us as He promised to be wherever two or three are together in His name. We two *are* together in spirit in the great mystery of God's spiritual kingdom, even though we are not together in body. Jesus therefore is with us, in as real a way as the air is with us even though we cannot see the air; as the wind blows upon us even though we cannot see the wind, even so the breath of His Holy Spirit breathes upon us though we cannot see that breath. Knowing therefore that He is here, I shall talk to Him:

"Lord Jesus, I ask You to enter into this person who has need of your healing in the depths of the mind. I ask You to come, Lord, as a careful housekeeper might come into a house that has long been closed and neglected. Open all the windows and let in the fresh wind of Your Spirit. Raise all the shades, that the sunlight of Your love may fill this house of the soul. Where there is sunlight there cannot be darkness. Therefore I rejoice that as the light of Your love now fills this mansion of the soul, all darkness shall flee away. And indeed in Your name I speak to that darkness, gently telling it that it cannot abide here in this one whom You have redeemed upon Your cross. Look and see, O Lord, whether there be any ugly pictures on the walls—pictures of old distressful and horrifying wounds of the past. And if there be such pictures, take them down and give to this memory-house pictures of beauty and of joy. So out of all the ugliness of the past make beauty, O Lord, for it is ever Your nature to make beauty. Transform old sorrows into the power to comfort others who have sorrowed. Heal old wounds by Your redemptive love, and turn them mysteriously into a love that heals the wounds of others.

"Go back, O Lord, through all the rooms of this memory-house. Open every closed door and look into every closet and bureau drawer and see if there be any dirty and broken things that are no longer needed in one's present life, and if so, O Lord, take them completely away. I give thanks, for this is the promise of the Scriptures: As far as the east is from the west, so far hath he removed our transgressions from us. (Psalms 103:12.) Look, O Lord, upon any memories that may come up from the deep mind as these words are meditated upon, and in Thy mercy fulfill in this Thy servant that forgiveness accomplished long ago on Calvary.

"Go back even to the nursery in this memory house —even to the years of childhood. Here, also, open windows long sealed and let in the gentle sunlight of Your love. Here more than anywhere, Lord, make everything clean and beautiful within. Take a broom of mercy and sweep away all dirt from the floor of this memory-room, even the confusion and the horror and the shame of ancient memories, perhaps of childish and uncomprehended sins, perhaps of the sins of the parents, those parents who should have been as God Himself to the child and who were not. Take a clean cloth, O Lord, and wash away all dust and wipe away every stain from the walls and from the furniture. Purge this Your child with hyssop, O Lord, that the heart may be clean. Wash this one that the soul which is created in Your own image and after Your own likeness may be whiter than snow. Look within the closets and under the furniture and see whether there be any broken and dirty toys, any old unclean rags of memory that are surely not needed any more at all in the adult life. And if so, O Lord, take them entirely away; gather them into Your own redemptive love, that the burden of them may rest upon the soul no more.

"Follow the soul of this Your child all the way back to the hour of birth and heal the soul even of the pain and the fear of being born into this darksome world. Restore in the soul that bright memory of Your eternal being that is not exactly a memory, but which is rather an emanation, an unconscious infilling of the eternal radiance from which this one was born. And if even before birth the soul was shadowed by this human life and was darkened by the fears or sorrows of the human parents, then I pray that even those memories or impressions may be healed, so that this one may be restored to Your original pattern, the soul as free and as clean as though nothing had ever dimmed its shining. Thus I pray, O Lord, that You will restore the soul as You made it to be and will quicken and awaken in it all those creative impulses and ideas that You have placed therein, so that whatever Your purpose may be for its human pilgrimage, that purpose may be fulfilled.

"'He restoreth my soul.' So said David long ago. 'He leadeth me in the paths of righteousness for His name's sake.' (Psalms 23:3.)

"I give thanks, O Lord, knowing that this healing of the soul is Your will and is the very purpose of the giving of Your life for us, and therefore it is now being accomplished and by faith I set the seal upon it."

7

The Healing of the Memories

I HOPE THAT THE SUGGESTIONS OF THE LAST CHAPTER have opened a door into the deep mind and that through that open door the Lord will walk back with you into the memories of the past so that they will be healed. How will you know when they are healed? When you can think of the very thing that used to trouble you so much that you closed the door upon it, and when thinking of it feel only a rush of joy, then that old memory is healed.

But what if it is not healed? If it is not healed, let us try something else. The unconscious mind is very timid. Probably it is not yet quite persuaded that such a grievous memory can be healed, or that so dark a sin can be forgiven. It has only your word, and you are too closely bound up with the trouble to speak the word with serenity, sureness and power. It has also the sound of my word from a distance. But that is generalized, of necessity, and read aloud from a printed page. I have great hopes of its therapy none the less, feeling that in a mysterious way it will carry with it an essence of power not only from my spirit but from the spirits of many who pray with me. However, I cannot guarantee that it will be sufficient for the healing of all of you, any more than a doctor can guarantee that a certain antibiotic will heal everyone.

But we need not lose courage, for we have not yet exhausted our resources. We read in the Book of Common Prayer in the Exhortations that follow the Communion service, "If there be any of you who by this means [the means of self-examination, repentance and reparation as suggested above] cannot quiet his own conscience herein but require further comfort or counsel, let him come to me or to some other minister of God's word, and open his grief. . . ."

Note in the above the connection between the conscience and grief. Note also the same connection in the Bible. We are told that Jesus died for our sins, yet we are also told in Isaiah 53:4, "Surely He hath borne our griefs and carried our sorrows." The truth is that any wound to the soul so deep that it is not healed by our own self-searching and prayers is inevitably connected with a subconscious awareness of sin, either our own sins or our grievous reactions to the sins of others. The therapy that heals these deep wounds could be called the forgiveness of sins or it could be called the healing of the memories. Whatever one calls it, there are in many of us wounds so deep that only the mediation of someone else to whom we may "bare our grief" can heal us. In the early church such a person was called a minister (one who ministered God's healing grace to another) or a priest (one who made the holy sacrifice for the sins of the people). And the act of going to him for help was called the Confessional or the Sacrament of Penance. This is simply the stylized manner in which the church through the ages has worked out a prayer for the healing of the soul, for the forgiveness of sins. In the Anglo-Catholic church the priest uses a confessional box for the same reason that it is used in the Roman Catholic church: for purposes of privacy. The penitent may see the priest in profile, but the priest cannot see him. The form of confession is printed on a card. The penitent states categorically that he has sinned, by his own fault, his own most grievous fault. This gives him no chance to say, "But So-and-So did thus to me" or "But the circumstances of my life . . ." or any "but" at all. The penitent further says, "I have committed the following sins," whereupon he lists those matters that lie so heavily upon his conscience that they have driven him to this difficult step. These things he confesses to God and in the presence of the priest. It is most clearly stated that he is confessing to God Himself and that the priest is only a mediator.

Why does he need a mediator? In many cases, of course, he does not. We do not run to the confessional every time we tell lies or lose our tempers. We note this deviation from righteousness and undertake with God's help to make it right. But there are times when the subconscious is so wounded with grievous memories that try as we may we "cannot forgive ourselves," as some are apt to say—that is, the conscious mind may accept a theory of forgiveness, but the unconscious does not believe it. In those cases a mediator has a most important duty to perform. The penitent says, "For these and all my other sins which I cannot remember I am truly sorry, intend to do better, and ask of you, Father, counsel, penance and absolution."

The penitent then rests his case and the priest takes over. If he has words of counsel he gives them. He then says "For your penance read Psalm Twenty-three and say the Lord's Prayer," or some such symbolic act. The penitent is supposed to kneel in a pew after the little service is over and faithfully do what the priest has commanded. And, strange as it may seem, even this small act of obedience is therapeutic! But the most important duty of the priest is to pronounce the absolution: to say that by his authority as a priest—the authority handed down all the way from Peter when Jesus said to him, "Receive ye the Holy Ghost: whose soever sins ye remit, they are remitted unto them; and whose soever sins ye retain, they are retained" (John 20:22–23)—he pronounces the absolution and remission of all the sins of the penitent. He does not himself by himself forgive them! And yet in a sense he does, for he makes the forgiveness of God through Christ real; he states it aloud in tones of such authority that the unconscious mind accepts the fact that they are gone. Therefore the burden of them is taken away, the grief of them is turned to joy and thanksgiving.

However, no service of prayer stands alone, separate from the faith of priest and penitent. The church may say that it does; that one saying a confession will go to heaven regardless of his sins and of the unworthiness and lack of faith of the priest. Well, so he may. Fortunately I do not have to decide the matter of what persons go to heaven. But this I know of a surety: the penitent is not necessarily completely released from the burden of sin unless the priest believes in what he is doing. I need hardly say, unless the penitent believes for, except possibly in a more authoritarian church than my own, he would hardly do this difficult thing unless he believed. He might, however, fail to make a good—that is, an honest—confession, and in that case the unconscious mind, knowing that he was lying, would not accept the release offered.

This is the stylized manner of bringing about that release which is the center and core of all Christianity; in fact, which *is* Christianity, the Gospel—the Good News that Jesus Christ is able to forgive sins. This can be done just as effectively in the informal manner: the troubled person coming to the minister and baring his grief—telling his troubles and sins—so that the minister can pray for him and thus create in his unconscious the assurance that these things have been turned into goodness and power, have been redeemed. This I know of a certainty.

At one period of my life the confessional was for me a very deep therapy. I was so fortunate as to be directed to a priest who believed in the forgiveness of Christ. Every Saturday afternoon from two until six he was in his small church on his knees, preparing his own soul to be a channel for this power. One penitent might come during those four hours, or possibly two. This priest did not feel the hours had been wasted, knowing that the saving of even one soul was worth all his time.

Later, however, on moving from that city, I did not find a priest so deeply and profoundly aware of the power of Christ's forgiveness. Although I still kept the rule of life learned from Father Weed, there was a lack somewhere. Moreover, memories kept arising, not so much of my own sins as of the effect upon me of the sins of the world seen and felt in my Chinese childhood. At this point in my life the Lord sent to me the minister of a Congregational church who had a divinely inspired understanding and faith, and through his quite simple and conversational prayers, release came.

The great trouble is that most ministers, having abandoned the formal confession as they abandoned so many things at the time of the Reformation, are unwilling to pray for the forgiveness of sins. They will try anything else! They will send the troubled soul away with specious statements that God is very tolerant and not to worry—and I have known of tragic endings to these inadequate sessions. "What did I not do?" the minister has wondered. The answer is very simple: he did not pray for the person; he merely told the troubled one to take it to the Lord in prayer (which he was not able to do, or he would not have betaken himself to the study of a strange minister).

I have mentioned the stylized method of the confessional, or the Sacrament of Penance. I have also written of the spontaneous method of telling our troubles to someone else, through whom God can give us the words of assurance or of guidance that will set us free. The one method does not exclude the other. To certain people under certain circumstances the confessional still has its power. But to other people and in other circumstances either it is not available or its power is dimmed by unbelief. Let us rejoice therefore that God cannot be limited by any form, but that His love still crashes through to reach us in ways both too great and too small for our comprehension.

So to you who need the healing of the soul and are not yet healed, I suggest that you pray for guidance, that God may lead you to one who is willing to hear your grief and to pray for it.

And, as in Chapter Two, I will now write to those who are standing firmly on their feet and who are therefore in a position to lift up the fallen. What shall you do if someone comes to you and wishes to "bare his grief"—in other words, to tell you about some besetting temptation or some old sin or some irrational fear?

Let me tell you as nearly as I can what I do myself. I ask him a little bit about his childhood. Then as he talks, I listen. I concentrate my full attention on him, praying that the Spirit of Christ will bring up from his memories whatever needs to be brought up, will guide him to say the key words and will help me to recognize the key when I hear it. Having prayed thus, I forget myself entirely. I am not aware of thought or feeling. I do not "pour out love" to this person, knowing that my human love is insufficient for his healing and might even become a trap to him. Moreover, to "pour out love" would be to have my mind on myself rather than projecting my whole mind and soul into the other person. Nor do I listen with any attempt to preach or moralize.

If the person says, "Yes, I had a very happy childhood," then I reply, "When did you start being unhappy?" Note I do not say, "What have you done that is wrong" or "You must be living in sin" or "You must not fear" or "You should have more love." Of course whoever it is must at times have done wrong. Who has not? But I have too much respect for people's souls to rush at them with any such question. I only give myself to them in the hope that whatever they have done may be forgiven through my sharing it with them, so that I can also share the life of Christ with them. Jesus had respect for their souls and died for them. Shall I not therefore accomplish the little death of laying aside my own life for a moment that I may enter into theirs? Certainly they should not fear. But unless the perfect love of Christ can be projected into them through me so as to cast out fear, they cannot help but fear. And the mere making up of the mind that one should not fear would only make them afraid to be afraid. Of course they should have more love. But this they cannot have because they have been so wounded in the past that even their power to love has been stultified. There is nothing more utterly discouraging to a person unable to feel love than the smug words, "You should have more love." It is as foolish as saying to an ill person, "You should have more health."

If the person merely tells me of old sorrows without giving the circumstances of his life that caused them, I ask another very simple question which can be encompassed in one word: "Why?" "Why were you so unhappy?" I ask. Or "What happened that made you feel that nobody loved you?" Or some such simple friendly query concerning his sorrows only and not at all concerning his sins. If the sorrows are connected with sins (as they usually are) this will come forth without my probing.

Sometimes I know that they are holding something back out of embarrassment or fear. And I wait, trusting for the rest to come forth as the Lord guides.

It might be better if I could more nearly approximate the methods of a counselor and could take more time for this work. But I cannot. Often—most often, in fact—I never see the afflicted person again. Therefore I must do the best I can on the amount of information given me. Fortunately it is not necessary for me to analyze and to know that *this* has caused *that* or something else has resulted in some other end. Very often indeed this connection is obvious; but, even so, I do not necessarily call it to the attention of the one for whom I am praying. I simply pray, usually with the laying on of hands, for the love of Christ to come into this one and forgive the sins and heal the sorrows of the past as well as the present—the little child who used to be, as well as the grown person who is now. I begin at the present and go back through the memories, mentioning every sin and every grievous incident that has been told me. Indeed, I go farther back than this, and pray for the healing of those impressions of fear or anger that came upon the infant far beyond the reach of memory. I carry this prayer back to the time of birth and even before birth and pray for the restoration of the soul, for the healing of the soul—the psyche—of the real, original person.

Very often the one for whom I pray says to me afterwards, "How did you know that?"

And I reply, "Because I saw it."

One makes a very deep rapport in this kind of prayer. One feels the feelings of the person for whom one prays; so much so that often the tears come from some deep center of compassion within the soul. Yet, if one weeps, it is not in grief but in joy, knowing that these tears are not one's own but are the tears of the compassionate heart of Christ brooding over this lost one, and the joy that interpenetrates the tears is the joy of Christ that at last He has been given a channel through which He can reach this person whom He loves.

For instance, I once prayed for someone in Australia who, though not by any means at the breaking point—the breaking point that I call an acute mental depression—was beset by sorrows over which he had no control and which hindered his efficiency. This troubled him the more because in his life at that time there appeared no reason for such a burden of darkness.

But in his childhood there had been a reason. He had lived very happily with three older brothers. Then the war had come and they had gone away. He had felt that he would never see them again. "I remember leaning on the gate," he said, "and watching them all disappear around the corner, and I thought my heart would break with loneliness. . . ." The brothers had eventually come back. But the security and joy of life had never come back until our prayer for the healing of the memories.

"I could see that little boy leaning on the gate!" I said, because I could, and whether that was visioning or imagination I do not know.

"Did you see him with a blue cap on his head?" he smiled.

I had to admit that in my visioning the blue cap had escaped me.

"Well, there was a blue cap on his head," mused the man, with such warmth of love in his voice that it cheered the heart to hear him. "And Jesus was beside him. But he didn't know it then."

The miracle had happened. The aura of feeling around the memory had been changed. From that time forth, the man would remember not a lonely and heartbroken little boy, but one who was protected and loved because Jesus was beside him. The child's sorrows had become a part of the redemptive love of the Son of God, and so they were redeemed and from that time forth they would be to him a source of joy.

How can this be? What is this most incomprehensible of miracles? Let me say only that it is *real*. And the findings of modern psychological thought have made it to some small extent comprehensible. For now we know that we have within us another mind than the conscious, and that this unconscious mind is not disconnected from life but is connected with the mind of the race: the collective unconscious. Therefore we can "pick up" thoughts and impressions from another or from life outside ourselves or from the memories of the race. Now into this collective unconscious, into these race memories, Jesus Christ entered, and there He lived during the days that we rightly call Passion Week. He made a rapport in the Garden of Gethsemane not merely with one person as you and I do when we intercede for another, but with all people who ever lived or ever will live upon the face of the earth: for He is from everlasting to everlasting and with Him a thousand years are as one day. When you and I learn to make rapport with one person for the purpose of healing, then we become connected by compassion with this one and we can reach his deep mind in prayer. Our Lord, when He took our sins and sorrows into Himself, made the connection with all of us. He became forever a part of the mass mind of the race, so that even though His living being is now in heaven at the right hand of the Father, a part of His consciousness is forever bound up with the deep mind of man. He has no tomb upon earth, for His body rose again, transformed into a different kind of body— one both flesh and Spirit. Yet in another sense a part of Him is forever buried within the hearts of men. When we realize the truth of His redemption and call upon

Him with such faith that the stone is rolled away and He can come out of the race-mind and be one with ourselves, then indeed the sin within us is put to death by the mysterious power of His cross and we are resurrected into new persons—new creatures in Christ Jesus—the new creation of God.

This may sound very obscure, very difficult. Never mind! Do it, anyway! True, understanding helps greatly, therefore I suggest that if you really want to set people free from bondage in this most wonderful way, you might pray daily for the gifts of wisdom and knowledge. For this "healing of the memories" *is redemption*. This is the the saving of the soul. This is the carrying on through Jesus of the work that Our Lord did for us on the cross. However, even without complete understanding (and who has complete understanding in this life?) we can still pray in this soul-saving way if we will but do it! This prayer work is directed by the conscious mind, reviewing the person's sorrows of the past and praying for the healing of each sorrow. But the actual deep therapy of the Holy Spirit is not done by us at all but by Him. And it is done through the union of two souls. It is not strange that we find ourselves knowing matters about a person's past that no one has ever told us. While the work is done by the Holy Spirit, the possibility of such instinctive knowing is already potentially within our natures. "Thought transference" it is called; the passing of thoughts from unconscious to unconscious. This takes place all the time. Occasionally, when it would be helpful, the unconscious pushes up unto the conscious mind as much as we need to know about a person. Thus in prayer for the healing of the memories, the Holy Spirit, working through us, quickens and enlivens a gift that is natural to us anyway. (In fact all the gifts of the Spirit are potentially within our natures.)

The gifts of the Spirit seem to me to be interlocked rather than sharply divided. This amazing knowing of that which we could not possibly know of ourselves is probably the gift of the "Discerning of spirits" (I Cor. 12:10) or at least one aspect of that gift. Moreover, since it darts back into the past in glimpses of matters that took place long ago and also forward into the future in prophetic pictures of the new person about to be born, it probably includes the gift of prophecy. And surely it is done in accordance with the gift of faith, as all the other gifts must be done. For in this kind of prayer we speak forth in faith matters that we do not know, being assured by the Holy Spirit that these matters are true.

I once prayed in Holland for a Dutch minister who had long been troubled and inhibited by the wounds of childhood. From the human point of view it was rather difficult for us to acquire an understanding of each other, for the interview was through an interpreter. It is hard enough to reach rapport with another even when a third person is present. (For this reason it is my custom to pray for a person alone unless I am so fortunate as to be with a very close prayer partner.) However, the Lord granted me sufficient understanding of the more or less usual childhood traumas.

He had been treated by three psychiatrists and was no better. He had also sought the healing of the church and had attended healing services faithfully . . . to no avail. The healing of the soul usually requires a deeper identification and a more profound understanding and sharing than can be had at any healing service.

I prayed one prayer for the healing of the memories. The interpreter said to me afterwards, "He say, how you know this?" And she mentioned a description that the Lord had prompted me to give of certain areas of his feelings.

I replied, "I know because I felt it."

This good man was healed. He returned a week later radiant with a new life and a new love. He had indeed known a breakthrough into glory, not the glory of a first meeting with his Lord and a first conversion, but the glory of a second meeting with Jesus and a reconversion that could truly be called rebirth.

How was this made possible? Because one person was able to go with him back through the years of his life and relive *for* him the sorrows of childhood. For the feeling that I felt was not that of the grown man. Until it was brought to the surface by my feeling it and putting it into words, the man had so repressed this particular wound that he did not in the conscious mind sense its pain. In psychotherapy the doctor makes the patient relive his past life, often with pain and with many tears, over a period of months. In the healing of the memories the one who prays relives it for him in the Holy Spirit of Jesus Christ, with a pain that is brief because the Lord turns it into peace, and possibly with tears of compassion but not of heartbreak. And, since the Spirit transcends time, there is no need for months of beating one's breast and reliving old sorrows.

A woman whom I will call Anne was once praying with a friend who was both alcoholic and mentally depressed. She prayed that her friend might be able to remember the very beginning, the root-cause of her trouble. After some moments of prayer the woman said, "I see a nursery—the room where I slept when a baby. But there's an empty place in the room. I cannot see what is there."

Anne therefore prayed that her friend might be able to remember what was in that empty place, to complete the picture that she was beginning to see. Whereupon, amazingly, Anne, remembering for her friend, saw in the empty place a crib and *was herself in the crib*. Then a huge face, red and terrifying, leered over the edge of the crib and Anne felt within her own heart the panic of the baby thus startled awake by a drunken father.

The depressed woman also saw the picture and remembered. "I was about six months old," said she. "And he bent over the edge of the crib. . . ."

Anne realized that the reason why the face looked twice its normal size was because she was seeing it through the eyes of a baby—and that baby was not herself but was the woman with whom she had merged her spirit, so that for the time being the two became one.

Anne once related this incident to a group that she was teaching. A psychiatrist, listening in amazement, grew as white as a sheet and gasped, "But that is depth psychology!"

Of course it is! Why not? It is the deep therapy of the Holy Spirit.

8

Lions in the Path

BUT IS IT NOT DANGEROUS TO CRASH INTO THE PSYCHE
of another person? Yes. Certainly. We are walking
through the jungle of life and there are lions in the
path. But it is far less dangerous than *not* crashing in!
And the dangers are not abstruse nor difficult, but are
the obvious dangers of any spiritual walk. The lions
will not hurt us if we are gentle with them.

The dangers are, first, that of being led away by
pride in our own prowess in healing and acting without sufficient Christian love.

Secondly, there is the danger of a misdirected love.

And, thirdly, there is the danger of becoming over-
stimulated—of overbalancing on the realm of the spiritual—of working too hard in spirit. This is just as real
a danger as working too hard physically or working
under too much mental strain.

First, then: do we really care for the person whom we would set free by prayer?

Fortunately most people who undertake this work do care; they have a sensitivity to the sorrow and the pain of others. They were born to suffer for and with others, and if they do not find a triumphant way of turning this aspect of their complicated natures into power, they might deem themselves queer beyond understanding. Some of them might be frightened of a tendency to share suffering, considering it masochistic or morbid, when actually it is only redemptive. Such people may rejoice and thank the Lord, for they are already enwrapped in the mantle of charity.

But there are some who fancy themselves as "healers" and who unconsciously derive a delusion of grandeur from thus entering into the holy of holies of another's soul. For instance, I knew a man greatly set upon and oppressed by a little group of these healers. They discussed him for hours in his presence, then decided that he was possessed by a devil and expressed themselves as horrified and revolted. They next said that they would have to see him again in order to cast out this devil. They gave him an appointment three weeks later, and forbade him to talk to his minister or anyone else until they had properly exorcised him. Whereupon, naturally, the man's last state was worse than his first!

This is, fortunately, most unusual. You need not be frightened, for you can avoid any such danger by the simple process of staying away from such a group. One moved by compassion would know that he could hardly do a work so sensitive and so delicate as the healing of the memories in the midst of a group. It would be like four doctors operating at once, but according to their whim: "Oh, let me take this out!" "No, no, you have it wrong—I feel another diagnosis coming up . . ."

What, then, was the matter with this group? They were not moved by compassion for the person who needed deliverance, but were led astray by their own intoxication with spiritual phenomena. Therefore they did not find the "key" to his trouble. So they fell back upon the devil, that most convenient alibi for all our failures in understanding. I have said before that the unconscious mind is open to influences from outside, and I have also mentioned the sad fact that there *is* a devil. It is possible that the primary cause of the man's disturbance was the infiltration of an evil entity from without. An English psychiatrist once told me: "A man may be rightly diagnosed as schizophrenic or manic-depressive, but this trouble on the surface of the personality may be caused by the infiltration of an evil entity from outside. And if this can be cast out there would be more hope of healing on the surface of the personality."

However, I cannot think that anyone moved by love would frighten his "patient" by telling him that he is possessed of the devil! If the patient himself says, "I feel I am possessed," then the patient has given him the key. Either he is possessed or he suffers from the fear of it. In either case, a person then may say a simple prayer of faith in the love of Christ, and may dismiss this troubling spirit, whether it be objective or subjective, turn it over to the compassionate hands of Christ, and then pray for the love of Christ to fill up all the empty places. And he may forbid any such entity or impulse—any such obsession of fear—to come near the person again and may surround that person with a circle of light. But if the person does not say that he feels he is possessed, it would be kinder not to tell him that he is! One could simply in silence or under cover of general words take the sword of the Spirit which is the word of God and command any unwholesome influence to depart from him.

Secondly, as there are those who oversimplify the matter of faith, saying, "Just say a little prayer and forget it," as though that covered the whole subject, so there are those who oversimplify this matter of love, saying "Love heals," and leaving it at that. Yet we all know mothers who love their children with an agony of love, and yet lose them. We all know wives who would die for their husbands and whose love has yet not healed them. Mere human "eros," good though it is, cannot do the work of God alone. Love is not the one and only gift of the Spirit: love is the mantle of all the gifts. Our human compassion opens a door into the soul of the other person, but into this open door there must walk the conquering Christ who alone can heal. He it is who once descended into hell and who therefore is quite at home in the deepest hell of our being. Without faith in Him and without the power of His Holy Spirit and the gifts of miracles and of prophecy and of discernment, the mere washing over of the person with a tide of emotionalism has little if any healing power.

One of the greatest problems is maintaining a right balance. Without love we can do nothing. And yet in order to be truly healing, our personal love should be merged into a self-sacrificial endeavor of faith and understanding—into a complete forgetting of oneself and into a deep concentration upon the other person. A mere "pouring out of love"—that is, an emotional reaction—is not enough and, indeed, can at times be dangerous. It can render the love of Christ of no avail by concentrating attention upon one's own feelings. On the other hand there are times when the one for whom we pray needs our personal "eros" as well as the "agape" of Christ. The Lord Himself can direct and order this love if we give ourselves to Him. For many years I formed a prayer habit of placing Christ between myself and the other person, and if I thought of my own feelings at all—which was unusual—it was only of sending my love to Christ rather than to the other person, that He might use it as He would. I could not send my love to the other person because temporarily I *was* the other person. This way of prayer is not recommended for all people, nor for anyone as a continuing method. It is praying through the power of the Cross. When one is filled with the Holy Spirit one no longer needs to do this, for one then prays through the power of the resurrection.

Thus the feeling of love that reached the sufferer would be the love of Christ and not merely my inadequate personal affection. Now that I have reached a certain age I have relaxed to some extent in this matter of protection. Protection is nevertheless an important consideration, particularly for ministers. A minister, wrapped as he is in an aura of holiness and often arrayed in becoming robes, is apt to stir the imagination and touch the heart of the opposite sex, particularly if they are of a similar age and more particularly if she enjoys the rather common feeling that her own husband does not understand her. Let such a minister walk down the bleak years with an attractive and doting female and he is in danger and so is she. Moreover, the wandering flame of eros that springs up between them is not necessarily the healing love of Christ, but can indeed be a tool for the delighted devil. It is a very real danger, but easily avoided by the following practical methods: unless dealing with a person much younger or much older, so that the difference in age is in itself a protection (for what minister of thirty would elope with a choir director of sixty?) the minister may, first, leave his study door casually open unless the choir is tuning up outside; second, avoid any physical contact save the sacramental gesture of the laying on of hands upon the head. He need not pat the lady or hold her hand or touch her in any way other than the one suggested above. Moreover, he need not speak of his love for her, even though he blanket it by saying, "I love you in Christ." Nor should he tell her that he needs her love. This unconscious seductiveness—this spiritual flirtation—is lots of fun for some people, but nevertheless is unadvisable. If the minister does not mean what the

pretty young lady thinks he means, she will later find
it out and he will be in trouble. If he does mean what
she thinks he means, he will be in worse trouble! If
both of them take it as merely a spiritual romp on the
edge of danger, then it makes a mockery of the love of
Christ and robs His stern and passionate redemption
of its power.

On the other hand, there are times when because
of difference in age or a stability of personality there is
no danger of a love that would cause trouble. And
there are those who need the warmth of human love as
well as the healing of the redemptive love of Christ. In
that case, an understanding of the soul of another and
a respect for that soul will guide us into a deep and
redemptive relationship if we walk cautiously. When
people charge upon me and tell me that the Lord has
informed them that I need their love, I tend to shrink
away from them. There is something wrong with such
love. It is too brash; it is too self-seeking; it does not
see into the heart of another or it would bide its time,
praying without words until it builds a bridge of understanding and of respect over which love may safely
walk.

Charity—*agapē*—the love of God that re-creates His
creation, is far more than affection: human love: eros.
It does not preclude human love and indeed in some
cases is greatly fortified by a feeling of personal affection. But in other cases this divine energy works with
more power when divinely impersonal. How can these
things be? Wherein lies the power that heals the
memories if it does not necessarily lie in the bonds of

human affection? It lies in and depends on the energy of the creative imagination which stems from love and is love—at a higher radiation and a more powerful wave length than the human mind can ordinarily encompass.

In other chapters I have spoken of the power of visioning. In the healing of the memories one must firmly hold in the imagination the picture or concept of this person as God meant him to be, seeing through the human aberrations or perversions to the spiritual reality behind them. Even though this person tells his deepest and darkest secrets, the one who prays must nevertheless see him always as a child of God, a saint of God, and turn in the imagination the dark and awful shadows of his nature into shining virtues and sources of power. Indeed, they can be thus turned. This is redemption!

The one who prays sees this from the beginning. Therefore the troubled person is able to tell things he has never told before. Nor is it the worst sinners who have these things locked up within them. Just as likely, so do the saints.

I once knew a young man greatly troubled by a homosexual drive. He went to the confessional, with how much deep conviction and how much courage God only knows, and sought the help of the absolution. But the priest—after saying, "Go in peace, God has forgiven all your sins"—promptly told him what a terrible sinner he was, intimating that he was not worthy even to set foot within the church. The priest did not really believe in the forgiveness of sins, which is really the healing of the memories: "Surely He hath borne our griefs and carried our sorrows . . . and with His stripes we are healed."

But can a homosexual drive really be healed? Of course it can! The life of Christ can enter into the memories, heal the childhood trauma that caused the little one to build a dam against normal feelings of interest in the other sex, and gently call all the feelings of love back to their normal stream bed, building high walls of protection on the right hand and on the left hand. This can only be done, so far as I know—and I have had hundreds of such healings—by the will and consent of those who are troubled by this aberration from the normal. I do not look upon this deviation as a great growly bear locked up in a closet. I look upon it as a harmless little Teddy bear, now about to be replaced by more adult toys. The troubled one knows my undisturbed attitude, without words, as one does know without words when one is accepted as oneself, regardless of one's sins.

Sometimes, but not often, this type of prayer takes the form of a conscious confession of sins, in which case I use the straight and direct words of the Bible and claim the promise of the Scriptures: "If we confess our sins He is faithful and just to forgive us our sins, and to cleanse us from all unrighteousness." (I John 1:9.) I do not state this promise in any kind of sacramental or churchly or professional manner, as though I were trying to be a clergyman. I only claim the right to give it as a Christian, remembering that all the promises are for all of those who call upon His name.

Most often, however, the person does not even think of his conversation as a confession. He is merely telling, for the first time in his life, the worst thing that he can possibly tell about himself. He is telling it because he knows that here is someone who can bear it. Also he knows that here is someone who will never, never reveal anything that is told. I do not need to say, "I won't tell anybody." Whoever needs to say that is very likely one already fighting the temptation to tell. Such a person, I need hardly say, should not attempt this high and terrible way of prayer—this deep and glorious way of the healing of the soul.

In these cases I often say afterwards, "But, you know, that is not your real self at all." And I describe the picture of the real self that God has helped me to work out of my creative imagination. This is often amazing, overwhelming, and most tremendously releasing to this person. That another human being could see him as a saint of God! Thus it is. One sees this by the power of the Holy Spirit and seeing it, one draws it forth. And this is the highest love there is: this is *agapē*, or the love of God made human.

Now let us consider the third danger not merely to this kind of redemptive prayer but to all of us who immerse ourselves in the world of the Spirit.

My minister son, who is my spiritual adviser in many matters, once said to me, "What about your shadow?" I did not know what he meant. But I found out.

What then of the shadow side that, as my son said, everyone has within him? Shall there be no shadow—nothing to dim the light of the ever-burning spirit within us?

Shall there be no shadow side upon this earth, that we should endure at all times the unendurable brightness of the sun with no cozy darkness wherein to rest our eyes? Shall there be no cessation of labor, that we must strain every moment in creativity? Shall there be no dimness between our periods of high joy so that the nerves of our bodies may rest?

We need a shadow side. I like to call it the balance wheel: this principle built into us that causes us at times to desire to do the exact opposite of that which we have been doing. When we have been to a prayer conference, for instance, we may come home thinking that we should remain on that high plane of prayer all the time. But we cannot. Our spirits are wearied with straining after God, just as the body can become wearied with straining after a football. We need to drop the ball once in a while and rest, so that the weariness may be healed and so that the knowledge and power we have gained may be planted deep in the subconscious, there to take root and spring up for the edification and strengthening of the entire being. If we do not recognize this need, if we try to force ourselves into conscious prayer at all times, one of several things may happen: we may have a breakdown of body or mind; or we may react with weariness and disillusionment to the whole thing; or we may develop certain nervous symptoms or mannerisms which, while harmless, are yet troubling to others; or, if we continually hold down this other aspect of our nature, it may explode into sin. There are those who wonder why a certain beloved leader elopes with the choir director. This is the explanation: he did not know his own frame; he did not remember that he was dust . . . as God most mercifully does! He did not realize that he had a human side as well as a spiritual side and that this human side, which wanted to forget all about God and play golf, was holy too in God's sight. It was wholesome: it was given him to make and keep him whole, lest he lose his balance while walking on the tightrope of this divine-human life. By forcing himself to lean too far to the right upon his tightrope, he fell out of balance and tumbled off on the left.

Now I am not suggesting that we rush from time to time into sin! But I am suggesting that we need experiences that are earthy, both work and play, in order to rest and refresh our souls. Ordinary work is a gift of God and a command, and is not to be denied without harm to the soul. "Six days shalt thou labor and do all thy work." Creative play is also healthy. Our forefathers did us no good when they branded various types of harmless games as works of the devil. It is possible, though I would not say common, for a person to become enraged and shoot a bridge partner, but that does not make bridge necessarily an evil game. It is possible for a farmer to take up a rock and hit somebody over the head even as Cain hit Abel, but that does not make farming evil.

I suggest therefore, most seriously, that those who

give themselves to this great work of prayer should not forget to play with people as well as to pray with people. It will not only keep them human but it will also keep them in touch with other human beings. From time to time I have taken part in amateur dramatics. I have not done so with the purpose of converting the cast! What a nuisance I would have made of myself! I acted Lady Bracknell in *The Importance of Being Earnest* or the kind lady in the play *Kind Lady* only because it was fun. (Given half a chance I would do it again.) But every time I have been in a play my mind has been chastened and illumined. First of all I have realized with dismay that I had forgotten how other people think! How can I help them if I grow so far away from them that I can no longer remember how they think? Secondly, there has usually been someone in the cast who came spontaneously to me for a bit of help. As we sat backstage amid costumes and borrowed furniture and grease paint we have laid aside our lines and talked about God. These wistful ones would never have let me pray with them if I had not played with them!

The greatest benefit, however, has been not to them but to me. I have entered anew into humanity. Moreover I have had a wonderful time, and the other part of my nature—one of the other parts—has had a chance to live and laugh. Therefore when I again betake myself to prayer, it is with an inner contentment and peace. My balance has been restored.

9

The Work of the Holy Spirit

WHEN WE HAVE SEARCHED OUR SOULS TO THEIR VERY depths, have brought up old sins that they may be forgiven and old sorrows that they may be comforted by the redemptive love of Christ, then are we completely healed in soul? No. Not yet. There is still the spirit of man: that center of divine life which I called in Chapter One the "pilot light" from which all the burners of creativity can be lit; from which, in other words, our latent abilities and powers are so swiftly brought into new life that we can indeed be called a new creation. This spirit in man is variously called by students of the mind the "Self" or the "Christ self" or the "supermind." I prefer to call it simply the spirit. This spirit of man is the original breath of life ("rhuah" in Hebrew) that God breathed into man when He differentiated him from other forms of life and made of him a living soul. It burns low within us all, does this transplanted spark of heavenly fire, this inborn awareness of our own nature as children of God. But while it is burning low it does not sufficiently light our way upon this earth nor warm our hearts worn with the long conflict of life.

We are not made complete in soul until this little flame is set on fire by the great flame of the Holy Spirit of God. "He shall baptize you with the Holy Ghost and with fire." (Luke 3:16.)

In my own life this awakening of spiritual powers came not in one all-enveloping flash but gradually, step by step. For, though I did not know the Holy Ghost, yet I was praying all along the way for the Holy Ghost. As I sought the gift of healing I was of necessity seeking the Holy Spirit, for He is the giver of the gift of healing. As I struggled to learn the prayer of faith I was working my way toward the baptism of the Holy Ghost, for the gift of faith is one of the gifts of the Spirit. As I earnestly sought for God's guidance in making decisions I was seeking the gift of wisdom. As I studied and prayed for understanding of that which I learned from the Bible and other books I was seeking the gift of knowledge.

But I became very weary with all this seeking and struggling. The Holy Spirit was *with* me, and strove through me to heal others. But the Holy Spirit was not *in* me.

The time came, therefore, when I was utterly exhausted and when the need for some new outpouring of the direct power of God was an overwhelming need. As I prayed together with two friends in like situation and like need, God sent a man to open my mind to the possibility of rebirth. He was not a minister but a doctor and a seeker after truth. He believed it possible that a flash of light from God could somehow awaken in us a center of light and a perception of God in such a way as to transform us completely; to accomplish, as it were, a sort of spiritual mutation. We had no idea what this might be, but his words gave us a sense of expectancy. We asked God how we should pray (having prayed long for healing, to no avail), and the words of God came to every one of us: "Pray for the Holy Ghost."

I have described this prayer venture in detail elsewhere, but I may here sum up the gifts of the Spirit that came to us at that time as follows: they were, I do believe, the very gifts that Jesus Himself promised and therefore the primary gifts out of which grew all the specialized gifts listed by Saint Paul. The gifts we became aware of at that time were: first, the joy of the Lord (John 15:11), which brought with it such a tingling of joy all over the body that we were instantly healed of our physical ills; second, the gift of the peace that passes understanding (John 14:27) because it does not depend on earthly circumstances, not the peace of inactivity but the peace of intense activity proceeding with smoothness and harmony; and third, the gift of truth (John 14:17), an inner power to guide one into right decisions and toward an understanding of things beyond the sight of man. I might compare these gifts to the three primary colors red, blue and yellow, out of which in various combinations all the other colors can be made. Moreover, when these three colors are combined in perfect purity then they resolve into the white light of creativity.

How can these things be? What is this mystery of the indwelling of God's Holy Spirit? We cannot understand it—not really. But let us go back to the holy mysteries of the life and death and resurrection of our Lord and let us carry our study a bit farther, unto the spiritual meaning and value of His ascension.

Jesus Christ, the concentration into spiritual visibility of the transcendent light of God, further concentrated and limited His being and became man. He became *a* man potentially when He was born of the Virgin Mary. But during the course of His passion week when He entered upon His great work of redemption in the Garden of Gethsemane and carried it through to the triumph of the cross, when He was so completely man that He even thought God had forsaken Him, during these days that shook earth and heaven He became *man*, mankind; one with the mass mind of the human race. Therefore since He became a very part of the collective unconscious of the race, when He died upon the cross a part of humanity died with him. We say this continually, we who are Christians, but we do not even begin to understand it. Some even say that we should die with Him, meaning that the "ego," or the "self," must die, that we must become holy automatons, without emotion or desire, plan or will . . . God forbid! If the ego dies, the soul dies. Jesus died for us not that our souls should die but that they should live! It is only our inherited drive toward evil that is potentially destroyed, so that if we claim this work of His for us, there is no urge of the twisted human nature that cannot be healed. This I know of certain knowledge for a hundred times and a hundred times a hundred I have seen it so.

But since He became a part of mankind, what did He do with us when He ascended into heaven? He did not cut the cord of love that bound us to Him. He was still man. He took into heaven His acquired manhood— so that a *man* forever sits upon the throne of heaven! And being man, He took us in a mysterious sense with Him. A certain emanation or an invisible and personalized energy of our spirits has already ascended with Him into the heavens. We might imagine Him taking the whole world in His arms and lifting us up to God and saying, "Father, here are these people whom I have redeemed; here is mankind, now reconciled to You because as I have become a part of them so they have become a part of me. I bring them back to You now so that You can once again fill them with Your Holy Spirit as they were filled before the dawn of history, when they walked and talked with You in the cool of the evening."

And I imagine God the Father receiving us again into Himself and making therefore a new merger of God and Man, a new sending-forth of the original Spirit of God, interpenetrating the redeemed spirit of man in a new way. "Finish then Thy new creation, pure and spotless let us be." So we sing in our old hymn on love divine. "If Christ be risen from the dead, then are we also risen with Him": so we read and sing on Easter Day.

Then why are we not a new creation in any perceptible way? Why do we still walk heavily? Because for this great transformation to take place in our hearts we must *open* our hearts. We must with understanding and faith ask the Holy Spirit to invade and fill us.

The choice is always ours.

When we three friends prayed for the Holy Ghost, God gave us a sign: a deep burning within the head, as though a spiritual power were awakening even the physical channel of brain cells, nerves, glands, whatever they might be, through which our power would increase.

The Spirit is power. Power moves. Jesus said in Luke 24:49, "And, behold, I send the promise of my Father upon you: but tarry ye in the city of Jerusalem, until ye be endued with power from on high."

My two friends and I had great need for this power, not for our own sake but in order to carry on the work of God. We were not seeking for signs and wonders and special gifts. We did not pray to speak in tongues nor to see visions nor to prophesy. We simply said, "Lord, we are washed up this way and if You want us to continue with Your work You will have to give us the power to do it. So now, if we heard You correctly, You said 'Pray for the Holy Ghost.' And we do. We don't know what this means or what will happen to us, but whatever happens, it is all right." In our ignorance, our approach was perfect. We wanted nothing except to serve Him better. In a way, though we prayed for the Holy Ghost, we were really giving ourselves to the Holy Spirit of God to use as He would.

And the first thing that happened to us, after the burning in our heads became perceptible, was that very increase of power: the healing of disorders that overstrain had brought upon our bodies, the release of burdens upon the heart, so that we could be quickened by that joy of the Lord that is life itself, the gifts of wisdom and knowledge coming to us through guidance, and an integration of spirit, mind and body, so that everything that we did could be done with greater ease and in less time.

The entering in of the Spirit was a rounding out of the full personality, a quickening of life in every area of thinking and feeling. The Holy Spirit is indeed the Life-giver, being simply the One through whom God in this day gives us His life. The gifts of the Spirit are not merely magic performances that God imposes upon us from without. They are—every one of them— the quickening and the bringing forth of powers already potential within us. Consider the gifts of the Spirit already discussed in this book.

The gifts of wisdom and knowledge: these are not imposed upon us from without so much as they are quickened in us from within. The power to use right judgment is a potential power of all of us, and when we make mistakes it is because, not knowing the Spirit, we do not listen to Him. The ability to learn is given to all of us in varying measure, for God makes no pretense of being what we would call "fair." He is interested in the whole pattern of creation and in a final plan which we do not as yet see but which requires a multitude of people, all different in their natures and in their abilities and in their talents. To standardize people, if we could ever completely succeed in this iniquitous aim, would frustrate His final purpose for life itself. The gift of knowledge is an integral part of our natures. It is increased by the Holy Spirit, both by the quickening of our thinking and also by direct information from without, in words or in dreams or visions or simply an inner knowing. There is of course danger in this, as there is danger in all adventure. We are likely in the beginning to mistake every voice within us for the voice of God, failing to realize that God has but quickened our ability to hear with the ear of the mind, so that we hear not only His voice but also at times something from the mind of another person or even possibly from the mind of the Enemy disguised as God. These dangers are greatly lessened if we realize that there are many voices in the world, in addition to the voice of God. A voice that tells us to do something contrary to the nature of God and at variance with His laws as expressed in the Ten Commandments, that voice is not from God.

Tommy Tyson said one time that God really took a chance when He spoke to Balaam through his ass. Because every time the ass brayed afterwards, Balaam might think it was God speaking.

The gifts of healing are also part of our nature. We instinctively know this when we place our hands upon a small animal or little child in order to give peace and comfort. By the Holy Spirit these gifts of healing are intensified, and the bit of faith that is in us is united with the faith of many and with the great flow of creativity that comes from the being of God Himself. Thus we are given a gift of faith. But it is not something imposed from without upon our natures but something already in us quickened by the increase of the Holy Spirit.

Even the gift of prophecy—inspired teaching combined when necessary with the transcending of time—is not altogether foreign to our nature. We are learning to see with the eye of the spirit as well as with the physical eye, that is all. We are learning to become aware of the larger world in which we really live. Some acquire this greater awareness through the fascinating study of science, postulating, proving, seeing with the eye of the mind that which cannot be seen with the human eye. Who has ever seen an atom or an electron? Others of us acquire a farther vision through the stimulating and awakening of our spirits by the Holy Spirit. In the larger world—the heavenly kingdom—time is telescoped; we are no longer under its dominion. Therefore when it is good, when it has a purpose, God allows us to see both before and after what we call time. We can enter into the accumulated thought vibrations of the ages, and feel the feelings and think the thoughts of someone who lived long ago. Many take this as proof of reincarnation but I do not so consider it. It is something both more simple and also more profound: we do not need to live again and again in time, for we live presently in *all* time if we did but know it. The vistas of prayer that this opens stagger the imagination! Can we send our prayer power back through time? Is this what Jesus did when He descended into hell and prayed for the spirits who were in prison in the time of Noah? (Peter 3:19–20.) Is this, to come down to something nearer to our experience, the explanation of the prayer for the healing of the memories?

How much greater we are than we have ever known! And yet in the face of the ages how infinitesimally small! We can but put our hands upon our mouths when we think of these things and repent, as Job did when he beheld the glory of God, even of this our humanity.

Not only does the Spirit of God quicken us in the gifts mentioned above and in those which I shall discuss in the following chapters—tongues, interpretation, the discerning of spirits, and miracles—but also in everything that we do. In fact, I do not believe that Saint Paul had any idea of laying down an exclusive list, saying "This the Spirit does and nothing else." As a matter of fact, in the same chapter, I Corinthians 12, he mentions in verse 28 those who are gifted in teaching and in administration and organization. In other words, the Holy Spirit *endues us with power*.

A young minister had been for years runner-up in a tennis tournament. After receiving an infilling of the Holy Spirit, he played a better game than he had ever played and easily won the tournament. The Holy Spirit had quickened his athletic ability—strengthening his body, quieting his mind, and effecting a better co-operation of body and mind.

Long ago I studied art and enjoyed doing tight little paintings about six inches by four, in hard pastel. Thirty years later I went up Mount Hood and was so intoxicated by the beauty of the mountains and snow and flowers that I could not rest until in some way I had caught it on paper. I found in a local hardware store some rough drawing paper and a box of crayon-like pastels, and started to work. "O Lord, guide my hand," I would say, being accustomed to doing everything by God's strength. The picture was twenty-two by seventeen inches instead of six by four, my expanded spirit no longer being able to express itself in a small painting. Even the "wrong" type of paper turned out to be right, the tiny depressions remaining like little dots of light and giving the picture air and space.

The Holy Spirit of Jesus Christ having entered into this world can enter and move within everything!

A successful and prosperous businessman once came to me in great perplexity. He had received a baptism of the Spirit and was troubled about his business. Should he leave it and go into the ministry? We prayed for guidance—for, indeed, there are times when the Lord invites a man to do just this, as he invited the rich young man in the Scriptures. But our guidance was that he should remain in his business, but give it to the Lord and ask the Holy Spirit to bless it and use it according to His will.

Last winter I saw this man again, after a number of

years. He had only one trouble: his income had doubled and trebled in a manner that embarrassed him, and he could not stop it. But the joy that he felt in his business was tremendous, for there he testified to the glory of God. He and his staff prayed for the guidance of the Holy Spirit in every decision. No man was hired except at the word of God. His factories were places of peace, for the Holy Spirit through the love of Christ so pervaded them that the heartbreak of quarreling did not enter in. Strangers entering his factories would stop and look around in surprise, as one sometimes does when entering a church, sensing a power beyond that which can be seen with the eyes. "What is it?" they would say. "I feel something here that I have never felt before. . . ."

How strange that we have tried to keep God out of our creativity and the work of our hands, when He is a creator and a worker, and when every factory and every school and every garden is of interest to Him! How strange that we have felt it unworthy to pray about such things as money, when Jesus Himself sent forth His silent word and even a fish of the sea brought Him that which He needed! All the money in the world is in God's hands! All the cattle on a thousand hills are His! Let us remind ourselves of this when we pray with joy and confidence for His Holy Spirit to move upon the affairs of this world and upon the minds of men and bring to us all that we need.

We have a right to expect this, just as any child has a right to expect that his father will take care of him. However, we do not ask it merely to have and to hold, but to use with wisdom and discretion for the peace of our families and for the service of God. In one sense we have everything, for God is our father and all things are His. But in another sense we have nothing, for we are bought with a price by the blood of Christ and we do not own even ourselves. Therefore we think of God's supply as flowing into us and out again into the world in His service. And as we ask Him to bless the inflow, so in His name we bless the outflow, giving our rightful tithe to His service and considering His will in all that we spend.

If we do this, the tides of life will turn in their courses and flow toward us. I have never known it to fail. And I have known miracles of the Holy Spirit operating through and upon money that would stagger the imagination. If I were to tell you the smaller ones you would think, "Of course, things like that happen; I needed twenty-five dollars and it came just at the right time . . . but I never thought of it as being a miracle." And if I told you the greater miracles in which money came to one's help from a source fully as strange as from the mouth of a fish, you would not believe me.

But remember, not only man is called upon to bless the Lord but so are all His works! "Bless the Lord, all His works in all places of His dominion; bless the Lord, O my soul." (Psalm 103:22.)

10

The Gift of Tongues
and of Interpretation

IN FIRST CORINTHIANS 12:8–11 ONE FINDS THE USUALLY
accepted list of the gifts of the Holy Spirit: the tools in
the tool kit with which we are to do the work of God
upon this earth. Some of these gifts have already been
discussed: gifts of wisdom and knowledge, faith and
healing and even prophecy or the transcending of
time. I have written of these gifts as they came to me:
in connection with doing the Lord's work. One might
remember that to the disciples also were given gifts of
faith and of healing before the day of Pentecost. (Luke
9:1.) When the Holy Spirit entered into them on that
day, there was already provided a channel through
which His power could work. One wonders what
would have happened to the disciples when such great
power exploded within them if they had not immediately channeled that power into works and words of
healing and of faith, using therein the wisdom and

knowledge of the Spirit! Read Acts 2, 3 and 4 and see how the power of the Spirit was extroverted into conversion and healing and the leading of a new life.

The gifts previously discussed might be considered the normal powers of a human being, simply enhanced and increased by the Holy Spirit. So they are. And yet I believe that even those gifts usually considered supernatural are not completely foreign to the human being, but are the explosion and extension of powers already latent within him.

But what about those gifts that are definitely peculiar and that some, indeed, consider actually psychotic: the gift of tongues and the gift of the interpretation of tongues? Surely that is something completely supernatural, given directly by the Holy Spirit of God! Yes, it is. And yet I believe that it is the explosion by divine power of abilities locked up in the unexplored regions of the unconscious being of man.

Yesterday I drove through the light of late afternoon just to refresh my soul with the beauty of the world. But the world was weary with winter. The earth lay dank and sodden among worn-out drifts of melting snow. The naked trees stood silent, waiting for spring. I passed an apple orchard that I remembered in full shining bloom, every old gnarled tree standing in violets amid the lush grass. Now the trees were empty. But they were not the gray of winter: their twigs and branches were a dim and lovely pink. Most people would not have seen that rosy tint. Some years ago I would not have noticed it, either. But through concentrating my attention not only on beauty that I should enjoy it but also on beauty that I should bring it to life in painting, I had sharpened my powers of seeing. I was not seeing something that was not there: I was seeing something that was there, but hitherto had not been quickened, by my seeing, into life. I was seeing not the dreariness of late winter but the wistful beauty of coming spring in those old apple trees. Yet the apple trees could not bring forth blossoms and fruit by themselves! They still needed the sunlight and the warm winds of April to bring to fruition the seeds of life that the Creator had built into them.

So it is with us. Even in the gift of tongues, the Spirit coming upon us from without quickens and awakens in us potential powers that the Creator planted in us long ago. For, from the beginning in the Garden of Eden, God has spoken to man. When man could no longer hear the direct speech of God, then the Creator spoke to him through the dark speech of dreams, moving mysteriously in the deep unconscious and often using symbols that the conscious mind does not comprehend till its understanding is opened. These symbols and dream images are frequently of great antiquity, coming out of the collective unconscious of the race. In days of old, men accepted the reality of "the dark speech of God" through dreams, visions, and the visitation of angels. They felt no need of an explanation, but simply believed that "God spoke to His servant in a dream" or that "God gave to His servant the prophet the gift of interpretation." Then came the age of reason and dream material was rejected as nonsense. Now in the new world of knowledge wherein we live, out of the nonsense emerges truth. This truth has emerged not in spite of man's urge toward understanding but because of it. Thus does all truth emerge: even the truth that the earth is round and not flat; even the truth that time is relative and that as we draw out of the pull of the sun upon its planets there will be no day or night, no summer or winter.

Now much to the consternation of many people, another truth is emerging concerning the mysterious working of God's Holy Spirit; namely, that He is able to speak both in and through an individual in a language that the person in his conscious mind does not know. This is called glossalalia, or the speaking with tongues. In the early days it was accepted by simple faith, as just another instance of the marvelous works of God. Then came the age of "reason" in which it was rejected as gibberish, as hysteria—quite a natural assumption if one does not understand the mental and spiritual laws through which this power works. But, with understanding, the matter clarifies and one can comprehend what really happens in the phenomenon and thus can judge wisely both of its very obvious dangers and also of its values.

Consider, therefore: the unconscious mind of man does not live alone. There is a mysterious connection between the unconscious being of one person and the deep mind of another. Moreover, this connection can reach back through time and forward through time and can make rapport with the thinking of someone who lived long ago or of someone who has not yet come upon this earth—and also, as the Bible repeatedly states, with heavenly beings who have never been inhabitants of this dark planet. Now in the speaking with tongues, this power latent in the unconscious mind of all people is brought to the surface and is quickened, so that the unconscious may make rapport with the unconscious mind of someone else living anywhere upon this earth or of someone who has lived before or of someone who will live in the future or even of someone from heaven: some great being, light-filled, whom God uses as a messenger of light that He may lift us out of darkness into the light of immortality. The person therefore under this inspiration speaks a language which the conscious mind does not know, but which *this deep area of the unconscious does know.*

A psychiatrist explained it to a friend of mine—Rev. Morton Kelsey, St. Luke's Church, Monrovia, California—in these words, which are all the more illuminating since neither the psychiatrist nor the minister had this gift, but were merely trying to understand it from the standpoint of their scientific knowledge: "It can be a spiritual power entering into a person with such force that it reaches and touches something in the deep unconscious; whereupon the person speaks a language which the conscious mind does not know, but which this deep area of the unconscious does know. I see that it can give a person great release, more than any number of shock treatments. But it is strong medicine and not to be administered lightly."

"Lay hands suddenly on no man," as Saint Paul

advised Timothy (I Tim. 5:22) for good and sufficient reasons.

Why? Why is it dangerous to rush upon an unsuspecting Christian with the gay remark, "Let us lay hands upon you that you may have the Holy Spirit and speak with tongues?" Or indeed, "Let's pray for you to get the Holy Spirit! Now (*after some prayer*) come on, *speak!* That's how the Holy Spirit comes to you!"

First of all, this is an inadequate concept of the coming upon a person of the Holy Spirit. I am very glad that when I first received the Spirit I did not even know that such a thing as the speaking with tongues existed in the present day. I am glad because in my excitement over this one rather dramatic gift I might have missed the real purpose of the Spirit which is to *endue us with power.* "But ye shall receive power, after that the Holy Ghost is come upon you." (Acts 1:8.) That is the word of Jesus. Power to do what? Power to become the new creation: the Sons of God. (John 1:12.) Power to do the works that Jesus did. (John 14:12.) The same power that Jesus gave to His disciples, the power to save the souls of men and to set them free from all evil and to heal all manner of sickness and all manner of disease. (Matt. 10:1.) One reason why the experience with my two friends had such great and lasting results was probably that we sought it for this purpose alone: that we might have the power to do whatever He wanted us to do. Not merely to have a spiritual experience—not merely to "receive the Holy Ghost" for our own joy and pleasure—but that we might turn whatever manifestation of power He might give us into service for Him.

This entering in of the Holy Spirit, with or without the gift of tongues, can grant to us spiritual blessings of joy and peace. Tragically enough, people have sometimes come to me, saying something like this: "I received the gift of tongues, but it didn't give me any joy. In fact, I've felt more depressed ever since. What is the trouble?"

The trouble is that someone, not understanding, "laid hands suddenly" upon this person before he was prepared to receive such an experience. Those who in their enthusiasm lay hands on anyone with a minimum of preparation probably do not know that while some are blessed by this, others are thrown into confusion and depression. I do know, for I often pick up the wreckage. And after they have been burnt over by such a premature experience it is much more difficult for them to receive the real, deep, life-giving power of the Holy Spirit. They were induced into a spiritual experience that they were not prepared to assimilate. This increases the cleavage between the spirit and the subconscious. It widens the cleavage in the personality. Now with some people, those sufficiently sound in mind and nerves, the Holy Spirit can do His own healing and balancing of the personality. But with others who are less stable emotionally He cannot because our own mistaken choice of procedure has made it impossible. Yes, I know with God all things are possible. It is possible if He so choose that He can alter His plan for this human race and make us automatons. But He does not so choose. He has given us free will and we are responsible for our own mistakes. He has given us His Holy Scriptures, and if we will read and obey we will not make the mistake of rushing into a spiritual experience or of inducing it in another without proper reasons and proper preparation. But if we do make such mistakes He does not overrule them for us. The Spirit endues us with power, but it is still up to us to learn how to use that power. *The choice is always ours.*

The right preparation, then, is in self-searching and understanding. Or in churchly language, in true repentance and the desire to lead a new life. And the right reason is that we shall receive power to do His work: that any energy released in us by this gift of tongues shall be used in building the new creation: the Kingdom of Heaven upon earth; not as an end in itself or merely that we may say to others, "I have the Holy Spirit because I speak in tongues."

Some people teach today that those who speak in tongues have the Holy Spirit and those who do not speak with tongues do not have the Holy Spirit. I cannot agree with this assumption. In the first place, the Bible does not teach it. "Do all speak with tongues?" says Saint Paul in First Corinthians 12:30, implying the answer "No." "Are all apostles?" he asks in the same passage. "Are all prophets? Are all teachers? Are all workers of miracles?" Thus he ends his great discourse on the unity of the body in spite of the diversity of the gifts of the Spirit (I Cor. 12:29–31) "That there may be no schism in the body," says he rather pathetically, considering the fact that the explosion of this gift *without understanding* has caused so much schism and controversy that many people wish it had been left safely wrapped in the napkin of ignorance and buried in the ground, as was the unused talent in Our Lord's parable. (Matt. 25:25–28.) However, Our Lord's remarks to the cautious one who primly buried the talent were not such as to encourage us in turning our backs upon an uncomprehended power. We would do better, as Dr. Henry P. Van Dusen says in his book *Spirit, Son and Father,* to seek the mysterious workings of the Spirit in spite of their occasional eruption into apparent hysteria rather than to reject the Holy Spirit in toto.

Another reason why I cannot accept the teaching that those who speak with tongues have the Spirit and those who do not speak with tongues do not have the Spirit is that it is not borne out by the facts of their lives. "The tree is known by his fruit." (Matt. 12:33.) "But the fruit of the Spirit is love, joy, peace, long-suffering, gentleness, goodness, faith, meekness, temperance." (Gal. 5:22–23.) Compare Ephesians 5:9 and James 3:18. I know many people who speak with tongues in whom these fruits are increasingly manifest. But I know others in whom they are not manifest. And I also know those who do not speak with tongues in whom both the fruit and the power of the Spirit are more observable than in certain ones who do speak with tongues. Therefore I believe according to the Scriptures that there are "diversities of gifts but the same Spirit," and that "the manifestation of the Spirit

•*179*

is given to every man to profit withal." In fact it is difficult for me to see, in the face of life and of the overwhelming testimony of the Scriptures, how anyone can teach that one *must* speak with tongues or he does not have the Holy Spirit. One may say that he does not have *all* the gifts of the Spirit unless he speaks with tongues. True enough. But the same thing may be said of the gifts of healing, of faith, of miracles, of the discerning of Spirits, and, most truly of all, of the gifts of wisdom and knowledge. Great harm indeed has been done by those who lack the gift of wisdom and who speak unwisely and publicly of the gift of tongues. If "there come in those that are unlearned, or unbelievers, will they not say that ye are mad?" asked Saint Paul quite as many persons ask today. (I Cor. 14:23.)

Saint Paul apparently took a dim view of the whole matter of using the gift of tongues in a public service. And if you search the Scriptures you will see no record of this gift being mentioned in a public service. Saint Peter did not say, "O ye men of Israel, ye must speak with tongues" nor did Saint Paul say, "Ye men of Athens, behold how we speak with tongues." In fact in the whole of the Bible one will not find these words: "You must speak with tongues." This gift was one that fell spontaneously upon a group of people prepared and waiting upon the Lord with great expectancy. (Acts 10:44–47.) On the day of Pentecost the Spirit came upon the disciples with such power that it shone forth to the world, both in miracles and in the gift of prophecy or inspired preaching and also in the gift of tongues. On that occasion the apostles spoke known languages, *understandable to the people.* If at that time the disciples also spoke in unknown tongues it escaped the multitude in the general excitement. Perhaps on that occasion the phenomenon of speaking in an unknown tongue did not take place. However there is such a phenomenon. (I Cor. 14:13–14.) And according to the Bible there is even a language from heaven. (I Cor. 13:1.) But these more mysterious gifts were to be kept for the edification of the saints and were not to be broadcast among those whom they might disturb nor to be imposed as a necessity upon anyone.

Saint Paul says, "He that speaketh in an unknown tongue edifieth himself." (I Cor. 14:4.) According to Webster's unabridged dictionary to edify means "to instruct and improve, especially in moral and religious knowledge; to teach." Those without understanding say at this point, "How can a man edify himself if he does not know what he is saying?" (It is strange that in this day of science and psychology so many people feel themselves adequate to discuss the mystery of tongues without knowledge either through experience or through study and observation.) As has been pointed out, he *does* know what he is saying. The conscious mind may not know but the unconscious *does* know. He is speaking forth for the first time the deep knowledge of that other part of himself and as he speaks it forth it is raised to a higher level of the unconscious, is grasped in the essence of its feeling (people so often say, "I just feel like I'm praising the Lord, and I feel so *happy!*") and sometimes even emerges into the reasoning mind so that a small peripheral part of it is interpreted in one's own language. No wonder one feels happy! I like to imagine the Other One in me saying "Hooray! (Or, in more appropriate language, "Halleluia!") Here *I* am allowed to speak at last!"

I am not against electricity because I may warn a grandchild not to stick a knife in the toaster or touch a hot iron. Those who go berserk over the gift of tongues have stuck a knife in the toaster and it is not the fault of electricity that they have done so. Those who speak of tongues unwisely, so that it has a destructive and divisive effect, have touched a hot iron.

The purpose of this gift is not that one should show off to others, but that one should edify oneself and therefore be better equipped to do the work that God gives him to do. Thus this gift is one of the tools with which we do our bit in building the Kingdom of God on earth. A good builder need not say, "Look at my wonderful tools!" One looks instead at that which he has built. How does one know that through speaking with tongues he has "edified" (instructed and improved) himself? Merely because he feels happy? By no means. Let us consider here another remark of Saint Paul's: "He that speaketh in an unknown tongue speaketh not unto men but unto God." (I Cor. 14:2.) He speaks directly unto God as did Adam and Eve in the Garden of Eden; his natural rapport with his Creator is restored; his soul is brought nearer unto God. A very holy man, Abbot Lazarus, of the Greek Orthodox Church, author of books on the mysticism of this church, once said to me, "I wish very much that I had the gift of tongues."

"Why, Abbot Lazarus?" I inquired, surprised beyond measure that this most erudite, British-educated scholar should desire such a gift.

"Because from my study in mysticism I have come to know that it would be a short cut to contemplative prayer. We spend hours every day saying the Jesus Prayer ('Lord Jesus Christ, Son of God, have mercy on me') in an effort to make contact with God. If I could speak with tongues, this contact would be made instantly."

Whether the Abbot has since received this gift I do not know, but I do not doubt at all that he is right in his deduction. Since one is speaking from the unconscious—or, as I would say, from the spirit—one is naturally in closer contact with the Spirit of God than when speaking and thinking through the dull medium of one's own language. Thus the edification comes from Spirit to spirit, and one perceives it through the improved ability to pray, to think, to write, or to invent mousetraps. Naturally. The Creator, speaking and operating directly in the unconscious, increases one's creativity.

There are some who say that one should not speak in tongues unless one interprets, confusing Saint Paul's advice concerning the use of tongues in a public service (I Cor. 14:5–33) with his statements concerning the value of this gift when used in one's private meditations: which value he does not explain other than by the verses quoted, but assumes as a natural thing demanding little explanation. "I thank my God I speak with tongues more than ye all." (I Cor. 14:18.) It is quite obvious that if tongues are used publicly there should be an interpretation, lest the unlearned and unbelievers say that one is mad. (I Cor. 14:23.) There should also be an interpretation so that the simpler part of the message may be broadcast, that all may receive it. I say the simpler part; for I am convinced that a great deal of those nuances of spiritual awareness that the unconscious mind experiences completely escape translation into words.

"Whether there be tongues, they shall cease." (I Cor. 13:8.) If tongues are a short cut to contemplative prayer—an entering into the great silence of God— naturally they will cease. Tongues when practised in private prayer are largely a way of silencing the conscious mind so that the spirit may be freed to commune directly with God. This is indeed the purpose of all contemplative prayer: to be immersed in God even to the exclusion of words. The conscious mind tries in every way possible to stop this, whether from the interference of the perverse principle within us or from the control habit of the conscious mind I do not know. We feel moved to pray for someone. We should rebuke that impulse and set it aside. Yes, it is good to do intercession, but not now. This is our daily meeting time with God. We may be guided to look up Bible verses. Let us close our minds to that impulse. It is good to seek guidance in the Holy Scriptures, but not now. God is waiting to speak to us in that inner communication that has no words, but He cannot until we sufficiently still the conscious mind. The mind tends to revert to the day's work. That is excellent after we come back to earth again, but not now! So those who have the gift of tongues do well thus to pray in the Spirit until their spirits find rest in that eternal silence that is yet pregnant with all sounds. For it is possible today as it was in the day of Saint John the Divine to arise into the heavens and behold things that are not lawful to utter. And in that heavenly kingdom communication between our spiritual selves there caught up into glory and those heavenly beings whom we may meet is usually not in words but in thought only.

All of this we lose if we permit the conscious mind to divert us from contemplation. All of it we lose also if we look upon tongues and interpretation as an end in itself and expend all our energy in talking!

Tommy Tyson tells a charming story of a boat race on the Mississippi. The old steamship *Oleander* always won the race because she had the biggest and fastest engine. One day the steamers lined up for the race and the *Oleander* was a-blowin' and a-tootin' and a-showin' off. They started. The *Oleander* got under way first. But when they rounded the curve and returned, the *Oleander* came in last. *She had wasted too much steam tooting her whistle.*

One reads in the second chapter of Acts a thrilling story of the first breakthrough of the New Creation—the merging of God's Spirit and man's spirit made possible through Jesus Christ, the Holy Spirit proceeding from the Father and the Son—when there were visible and audible signs of a miraculous power at work, as there were when Our Lord was baptized. (Mark 1:10–11.) However, although the disciples did meet together from time to time in prayer and worship, the focus of interest shifts immediately to the *results* of that miraculous descending of the Holy Ghost; to works of power: inspired preaching or "prophecy," the healing of the multitudes, the founding of a church. Pentecost was not the end. It was the beginning.

There have been many revivals throughout history, with or without the speaking in an unknown tongue. One reads of churches full of people being convicted and converted by the Holy Spirit; staying in the church all night with prayer and weeping, confessions and tremendous spiritual stimulation. But what are the end results of these revivals, other than the "saving of the souls" of those involved? The end results of Pentecost were the turning of the world upside down—the shaking of the Holy Roman Empire itself—the founding of a worldwide church. *The power of emotion was turned into action.* Long ago when I studied psychology I learned from William James that any emotion not turned into action is useless or even dangerous. A friend of mine was in a small group wherein one youth received the Holy Spirit with the gift of tongues amid considerable emotion manifesting itself in tears, trembling, and so forth. "You're getting overcharged!" said my friend in tones of authority. "Turn around and lay your hands on Joe and pray for the healing of his ears!" So the young man did. His friend's hearing was improved. The excitable young man was quieted and the power within him came under control.

This concept will be unpalatable to some readers who make a fetish of holy joy. Nevertheless I return to the purpose of all our Christian walk, which is not simply the acquiring of joy but which is to be Christ's faithful soldier and servant and to fight manfully under His banner against sin, the world, and the devil. (The Order of Holy Baptism, Book of Common Prayer, page 280.) True, the first experience of the Holy Spirit whether with or without tongues does fill one with joy as does one's first experience of falling in love and finding one's love reciprocated. It is a holy marriage and the joy of it can be so great that it is comparable to a high state of inebriation. (Acts 2:13–14.) But even as in an earthly marriage, when one undertakes the responsibilities of this new relationship the ecstasy is apt to be quieted except for occasional moments, and the holy joy is apt to turn into a steadfast using of the power of the Holy Spirit in doing the works of Jesus Christ. Those who seek nothing except their own satisfaction are like a young couple who refuse to take on the responsibilities of marriage—work, a home and children—but who desire only moments of ecstasy without the creative results toward which that God-given urge to love should move.

On the day of Pentecost the multitude heard the disciples speak to each one in his own language: an amazing number of languages. (Acts 2:6–14.) When Saint Paul advises the Corinthians concerning the discreet use of this gift of tongues he repeatedly speaks of an *unknown* tongue, stating explicitly that the multitude would not understand what was said unless there was one to interpret. There are, then, two ways of interpreting: one by previous knowledge of the language and one by the direct inspiration of the Spirit. Do such things as this happen today? Yes, they do. Often in a group one person will speak and another will interpret. I know an instance of a group attended by a seminary professor. He did not possess this gift, but being a teacher of the Bible he was interested in learning whatever he could learn of the operation of the Spirit—as indeed every teacher of the Bible should be. It happened that a young woman spoke in tongues, the voice becoming clear and loud, and the words going forth in a tone of authority. The group naturally became silent. When she had ceased, another woman spoke forth in English. The professor said afterwards that the first young woman had spoken perfect Hebrew and the second woman had given a very fair interpretation—neither one of them, of course, knowing Hebrew.

Why did the Spirit of God so move upon this group? The answer is self-evident: in order to illumine the mind of the visiting professor. From that time on, when teaching the stories concerning the gift of tongues, the teacher was able to say, "This is true. It happens today. I heard it myself." On this occasion tongues were for a sign to one who did not believe, but was willing to learn. (I Cor. 14:22.) And note that both methods of interpretation were used: one interpreted by the inspiration of the Spirit, not knowing what she said, and another interpreted by a previous knowledge of the language.

I have said that in one's private prayers, one who is filled with the Spirit is apt to speak briefly with tongues and then to enter into a state of high contemplation. Perhaps this is why Saint Paul found the gift so valuable. At the end of this contemplative period, one finds one's thoughts spontaneously returning to the earth again. The duties of the day come back to mind, but with a feeling of zestful interest rather than with weariness and dread. One probably listens for any message that may come from God in one's own language and writes it down. This is not the actual voice of God speaking to us in English or whatever our language may be. It is the unconscious mind trying to get across to us some little bit out of the great mysteries that we have briefly touched in spirit. The thought that comes to us in words may be a strengthening and uplifting message or a bit of illumination as to some question that has been in our minds. Or it may be direct guidance as to the day's work or even a bit of prophecy concerning future events. I do not know whether this message in comprehensible words is the interpretation of tongues or whether it is simply a thought coming from God. But this I know: whatever it is, it comes "through a veil darkly"—through the veil of the limited understanding of the conscious mind. It is only a small fragment of that which the unconscious has been hearing and feeling. Thus it is possible for the ego to distort the guidance, projecting into it something of one's own wish or self-seeking. We should therefore subject this guidance to the test of common sense and also to the guide rule of the Ten Commandments. If it is contrary either to the laws of God or to the laws of life, then we should not take it as an irrevocable rule for action but should seek guidance again, both directly and also possibly through consultation with others.

Finally we should never make the mere seeking of guidance the purpose and object of our communion with God, for then we limit God. He may have for us some illumination far more important than the mere question of whether we should or should not accept a certain invitation. Our guidance is like the postscript to a letter. The real script of the God-to-man communication cannot be framed in words. So, if one's attention is focused too completely on words, even the words of guidance or interpretation, one may cut short that real communication which is the object of this divine indwelling.

But if one forgets oneself completely and fixes the mind upon God, letting the words that come unbidden to one's lips flow as they will, then this gift can be most wonderfully therapeutic in the healing of the soul. For out of the depths we cry unto the Lord and the Lord who dwelleth within the depths hears our cry and His love flows over us in a way we have not known before. Moreover, when we do not know how to pray, then the Spirit within us prays with "groanings that cannot be uttered," or, as we might say, with sounds that cannot be expressed in our own language—and we have a serene knowledge that out of the deep unconscious we are praying according to the will of God. And from the feelings that accompany our prayer we sense that we are being lifted up more closely into His being than we have been when tied to the chains of our own understood tongue.

Thus the door of the soul is opened more widely and the King of Glory can come in. And while He does not, even with His Spirit, make us instantly and automatically perfect, the choice being always ours, nevertheless the Spirit moves within us toward perfection, such being the will of God for us. So it is that Saint John is able to say, looking forward hopefully to that which shall be, "Whosoever is born of God doth not commit sin." (I John 3:9.)

11

The Discerning of Spirits

THE GIFTS OF THE SPIRIT ARE NOT PUT UP IN SEPARATE compartments or isolated in cellophane wrappings. They weave together and work together in a natural manner. The gist of the matter is simply this: the Holy Spirit of God being awakened within us enlivens and enlightens our spirits, bringing forth in us increased power in every way according to our need and according to our desire.

Among the first gifts of power that Jesus Christ gave to his disciples was that of the discerning of spirits and being in control over them. (Luke 10:17.) We have already considered the gift of the discerning of spirits in its application to the discernment of the deep minds of living people so that we can more effectively pray for the healing of the memories. Now let us consider this gift in its application to the work of exorcism: the discerning and casting out of an evil spirit.

How can a spirit foreign to our natures take over our personality? Is it possible that deviation from the norm of human speech or behavior is actually the work of an invading spirit?

Yes, it is possible, and this can be the manner of it: we can indulge ourselves in a certain destructive feeling, let us say a feeling of anger, until it becomes a habit with us. This spirit of anger can spread and grow until it transfers itself to others who are not the original cause of our wrath and we find that they also irritate and enrage us. After a while this spirit of anger—this house of anger that we have built within us—can so take control that we are not our real selves. At first we had the anger. Afterwards the anger has us. It has become, as Jung says, an "autonomous complex" . . . a habit of thinking that has taken on a life of its own. Up to this point this is not the infiltration of an evil spirit or what people are apt to call "possession." It is something within ourselves. And, as soon as we are sufficiently out of depression to do so, it is up to us to look within, to trace its cause or causes and to correct this bad temper that from time to time takes over our personalities.

For bad temper is a sin. The one who curses his brother has in effect pronounced a curse upon himself. (Matt. 5:22.) The one who hates others does harm both to the souls of the others and to his own soul; for God is love, and hate is contrary to the nature of God. The mother who snarls at her children in tones of viciousness is sinning against them.

However, this thing can go one step farther: according to Carl Jung, there are actually outside entities or thought currents of evil, and it is possible that one of them will enter and live in this house of anger that we have built, so that in truth we are troubled—or, as people say, "possessed" by an evil spirit.

The word "possessed" is in quotation marks because, while it is the common expression for certain disturbances of personality, I am not sure that it is quite correct. True, in ancient countries such as China with their long history of evil and the fear of evil (mingled wistfully with much charm and real goodness) there are cases of personalities so taken over by something not themselves that they speak in the third person and act in a way that is totally contrary to their real nature. My father, the Reverend Hugh W. White, wrote a book on such matters: *Demonism, Verified and Analyzed.** In it he made the interesting statement that he did not believe that phenomena such as he had seen and dealt with in China were possible in a Christian country. Up to the present I am inclined to see truth in this remark and can only trust that this country may remain sufficiently Christian so that this may continue to be true. So, while I may use the word "possession" because it is in common usage, it is a joy to point out that one who has given himself to Jesus Christ cannot be completely possessed by any other than Him. Even if the powers of darkness have got hold upon him to his great distress, nevertheless, Jesus Christ still has a hold as well. And if he persists

* This book may be secured from University Microfilms, Ann Arbor, Michigan.

in faith and in seeking the power of the Holy Spirit, either his own control will increase until he can say to the encroaching enemy, "Get thee behind me, Satan," as Jesus Himself did, and be set free, or the Spirit will lead him to someone who can set him free. This setting of a person free from the encroaching evil is called exorcism and has of course been known in the church from the beginning. And interestingly enough, the word that Saint Paul uses is "the *discerning* of spirits."

To use exorcism without discernment is to precipitate more trouble than we heal. There is, here as elsewhere, the danger of oversimplification: of merely attributing every dark thought or mood to "the devil" and trying to cast it out. Sometimes it is not the devil at all, but is the emergence from the unconscious of some subjective problem, such as the one of anger, with which we ourselves should cope; it is the shadow part of ourselves needing recognition, understanding, and adjustment. In this case, if we leap lightly into a command prayer, telling Satan to go away from us, we are merely closing a door to the inner self that God has been trying to open for our consideration.

On the other hand, there *is* an evil power and there are evil or ignorant entities working on the plane of that power. And it may enter into us in other ways not at all as an outgrowth of our own self-built "house" of hate or fear or lust. One way in which this power finds an open door in us is the way of spiritualism. And I write this not theoretically but on the basis of practical, experienced knowledge. In other words, I have known it to happen. Why?

Hear the words of a minister to a friend: "I have been the route of mediumism, Rosicrucianism, gnosticism, mysticism, and nearly every other 'ism' I could find in my search for the power the church so desperately needs to deal with today's world. But having been, I am very concerned for you, for I know firsthand what can happen to you as you search. I am glad you are aware that you can get possessed. . . .

"This business of higher spiritual matter is particularly difficult to walk in. Let me show you how things become twisted. Of course God can work through benign spirits and souls of the departed through mediumship to effect some cures! Edgar Cayce must surely have been such a case. But that does not ipso facto justify mediumship even if benign. Of course God works through angels and saints, but we are to contact deliberately only one departed person, the Lord Jesus Christ. He will never in any sense 'defile' us (as in Lev. 19:31). He is the only departed one who has been perfected here; therefore the only one it is ever completely safe to contact. Then, when we do contact Him in prayer as we ought, He is able to send angels and saints around us and with us and I dare say sometimes to speak and act in and through us to get His and our will done.

"Just as in the world there are many benign persons who have never fully come into subjection to our Lord, so there are in the spirit world, many benign persons who, like the people on earth, do not realize at what points they are not yet fully surrendered to the Lord. Thus they want to work and serve, but in higher spiritual matters they sometimes get confused and tempted. So even though we contact a very benign person on the other side, we get 'defiled' to the extent of his or her imperfection. That is why Isaiah says in Isaiah 8:19 'Should not a people seek unto their God?' There is a proverb which says, 'There is a way which seemeth right unto a man, but the end thereof is death.'

"Let me tell you what else can, and sometimes does, happen. You see, we are to ascribe all glory and majesty and honor to the Lord. We are to turn to Him for *all* things. He will tell us whatever we need to know. But He will never tell us what it is forbidden for us to know, because He has been perfected here in wisdom and obedience. 'Yet learned He obedience by the things which He suffered.' (Hebrews 5:8.) He will never defile us with the first sin of eating forbidden fruit of the tree of the knowledge of good and evil. But when we contact other spirits, however benign, we can be told information forbidden to us. And then gradually we can be turned, until the spirits we spend the most time with are not the Holy Spirit but the other spirits. God says in His word, 'Thou shalt have no other gods before me.' The Holy Spirit will tell us all we need to know. A man baptized by the Holy Spirit can talk with God, hear Him, and obey Him. Why should we turn aside to false gods (however benign)? Not only can a spiritist 'healer' thus subtly be turned until he follows the guidance not of God's Holy Spirit, but of other spirits not fully under His control, but he then unwittingly leads others astray. Mediums may be sincere, but sincerely wrong!

"You say, 'I do not think that it is for us to dogmatically decide how God should run His own affairs.' If you say to a man 'Do not steal that car,' are you 'dogmatically deciding how God should run His own affairs?' It is not you who has decided that a man ought not to steal. God *has* managed His own affairs and said in His word, 'Thou shalt not steal.' Just as clearly again and again God, managing His own affairs, has said 'Do not turn to mediums or wizards.' Look it up in your concordance. Look up the word 'medium.' I challenge you, find *one* place where God does not speak of mediumship as abominable! If you want another shock, look up 'abominable' and you will find listed again and again as the 'abominable evil practices' the consulting of mediums.

"Now one final warning, when you pray, you open your whole body to the Lord; your whole psyche, mind, heart, body, and strength become more readily able to attune to Him and be used of Him the longer you practise prayer. Do I need to complete the analogy? To whom or what are you training your body and all within you to attune? What psychic and spiritual channels are being opened that ought to be closed? To whom are you attaching yourself?

"To be a prisoner to Christ is to be really free. 'I can do *all things* through Him who strengthens me.' Why should I defile myself with any spirits less than His? The secret of power is the secret of the baptism of the Holy Spirit. Demonstration in the Spirit and power will come through infilling by Him, and obedience. There are no short cuts or other ways, 'Whoever is not with me is against me.' Which are you, with Him or against Him?"

Therefore in conclusion let me say: if after I have gone to heaven someone tells you that he or she has a direct connection with me and that I speak through her and give her messages as to what you are to do, believe her not! She may be sincere, but if sincere she is deluded by some other spirit than my spirit. When I have gone on to another world, I will continue to pray for you, but I shall not return to contact you.

There are many miscomprehensions concerning this matter among Christian people. "But I am so spiritual," some think. "It cannot hurt me!"

Experience has shown me that there is more danger to the very "spiritual" person than to the earthy one who is merely seeking pleasure on the psychic plane. For the one who is really spiritual is unconsciously mixing a higher voltage of spiritual energy with a lower voltage; or, one might say, is mixing two different currents of power, as if one mixed the alternating current of electricity with the direct current. This adds danger not only to the one who seeks to find spiritual power through mediums but also to others in the group.

Again, some people say, "But I surround myself with protection in the name of Jesus Christ!"

This does not work, either, as Jesus Himself pointed out when tempted to throw Himself from the pinnacle of the temple and trust to the protection of God to save Him. According to the words of the minister quoted above, dealing in spiritualism is disobedience to God and therefore one cannot indulge in it and be protected merely by mouthing pious phrases.

Now let us consider the matter of the autonomous complex and of the real infiltration of an evil spirit. How shall we differentiate between them so that we do not run about lightly casting the devil out of everybody?

The most difficult part of this otherwise quite simple prayer is the diagnosis: hence the biblical words, "The gift of the discerning of spirits." When we perceive them correctly, then we have the power and the knowledge to cast them out.

How shall we perceive them? The gift of discernment sometimes causes one to "see" a picture within the mind of a face whose expression denotes its character; so that one can say, "You spirit of fear, I cast you out" or, "You spirit of lust or death or anger. . . ." Some people have this gift to a marked degree so that one does not know whether they actually perceive an indwelling entity or whether the Holy Spirit reveals truth to them through a mental picture. Another and more common way of perceiving is through the conversation of the troubled one. In fact a very good rule is never to go into a vocal prayer of exorcism unless the sufferer himself indicates in words that such is his need. They do this more often than one would think. "I just feel like I'm possessed," they say—and usually we ignore it, merely saying, "Oh, now, my *dear* . . . !"

If someone says this to me, I reply "Good! Now we

know exactly how to pray. For Jesus has given us power over all manner of devils and if something is possessing you we will just tell it to go away!" (May I add that even if the person is not really possessed, this prayer approach has great power because it is simple, direct, and in line with his own concept of his trouble.)

Sometimes, if I judge the trouble to be "possession," I lead the person into admitting it. There was a woman, for instance, with the usual persecution complex which just might be called a persecuting spirit. I said to her, "Where do these voices come from? Do you suppose you are imagining them?"

"Oh, no!" she replied, as I knew she would. "I hear them. They are after me! They follow me!"

"Well, then, do you suppose they come from God?"

"Oh, *no!* Because they are bad—they are terrible!"

"Well then, if they don't come from you and if they don't come from God, where do you suppose they come from?"

"It seems as if they come from the devil! I've always felt that but nobody believes me."

I believed her. So I took a long chance and commanded them never to speak to her again—and so far as I know, they never did.

And I followed this command with a general prayer of exorcism after my usual pattern, which is as follows:

First of all I pray, usually in silence, for myself and for this person to be surrounded with protection.

Secondly, with or without the laying on of hands, I

command the invading spirit in the name of Jesus Christ to leave this person. I continue this command and exhortation with any words of power that come to mind, holding up in my imagination the cross of Christ and taking the sword of the Spirit which is the word of God.

Third, I give thanks that the evil spirit has departed. Often I sense this very definitely, but even if I feel nothing I give thanks anyway as an act of faith. And I direct this departed thing into the hands of Christ who will know how to deal with it. I do not condemn or hate it, for there may be something in it which can be saved. I only place it under the control of Christ, and forbid that it shall ever come back to this person or to anyone else or to the earth plane at all.

Fourth, I pray that the love of Christ will come in quickly and fill up all the empty places where this used to be.

And finally I pray that the person may be surrounded from this time forth by heavenly protection so that nothing can come near him to trouble him.

This is really a battle against the forces of spiritual wickedness in high places (Eph. 6:12), and needless to say, one should never attempt it unless one serenely feels the power. A minister, if only he believes the truth of it, can always do this work, for the authority is passed down to him in his ordination and the devil knows it. But not every lay person is sufficiently endued with power.

That all this may become concrete, let me illustrate it with a case history.

There is a woman, now a grandmother and a missionary in India, who for many years was driven and compelled—or almost compelled—toward suicide by an inner compulsion that she called simply "the beast." This came upon her when a child for reasons that I do not know. She went to the railroad one day planning to throw herself under a train when Jesus through one of His faithful followers saved her . . . for the moment. The woman who spoke to her and unwittingly diverted her attention from this plan was a Bible class teacher. She said to the girl, "Oh, I've been meaning to ask you whether you would join my Bible class." Then, looking at her again, she said, "I beg your pardon. I mistook you for someone else! But I would be very happy if you would come."

Years later however, this sufferer, who had married a medical doctor missionary to China, became more and more overwhelmed by this "beast." The atmosphere of a heathen country, filled with the fear of every kind of dark force, naturally compounded her trouble. Time after time she was stopped by someone as she was about to throw herself off a cliff or into a canal. At last, one day, a voice spoke in her heart and she knew that this was the voice of the Lord. "I am not going to pull you back from another cliff," the voice said. "You must tell your husband of this trouble so that he can seek help for you."

She did so. But unfortunately there was no one who recognized the nature of her trouble or knew that a prayer of exorcism was needed. This is strange, for many missionaries did this type of healing for the Chinese. But, as I have said, the symptoms of the Chinese who became really possessed differed from the symptoms of this lady who, although driven and tormented, was still held fast by her Lord. However, she was at least protected from doing damage to herself and shortly afterwards the family was evacuated from China on the liner *Gripsholm,* along with many others. The dislocation from the only home she knew and the shock of adjustment to a new country did nothing to help her. She was committed to a mental hospital and her husband was advised to forget her, take care of his four children and make a new life for himself as best he could. At this point he began to study Freudian psychiatry and became an analyst as well as a medical doctor. His wife, after many shock treatments, was sufficiently quieted to be allowed to come home, at least temporarily. In spite of everything Jesus held on to her and she knew that some day she would be healed. She was taken at one time to a minister that he might pray for her the prayer of exorcism. However, unfortunately he did not remember that Jesus gave to His disciples power and authority over all manner of spirits nor did he know that this power remains to those who call upon His name. He said the prayer because he could not refuse, but it was not effective.

Her husband later brought her to a conference where I was lecturing. He learned to his dismay that I was not taking personal appointments, as I deemed five days to be insufficient time to care for the souls of four hundred people. Still the Lord maneuvered—

manipulated, if you like—to perform His will and in a very simple way: these people sat beside me at the first meal and indicated their difficulty. Of course I made an appointment to pray for her.

I will never forget the occasion, for it seemed as though every power in hell strove to prevent our prayer. In spite of all, however, it did take place. The final block came from the lady herself: "Do not pray for exorcism," said she, "for someone did pray for it once and it failed and I could not stand another failure."

This was one of many occasions on which I have prayed an exorcism prayer in silence. I informed the spirit of death within her that it could not possess her no matter how hard it tried, and that it was now to leave her. I took it by faith that God's words could not fail and that this troubling spirit was departing. I held up in my mind the cross of Christ before it and speeded it upon its way. I then turned it over to Christ, placing it in His hands and asking Him to do whatever was best with or for it. But I commanded it never to return to this woman. Finally I prayed aloud for her to be filled with the love of Christ, thinking to myself, "All the empty places where this used to be are now being filled with the love of Christ so that nothing can ever again enter into her to trouble her." And I prayed for the protection of the Lord to be round about her like a circle of light.

She was healed. The healing was so quiet she did not realize for several days that the "beast" was gone. She remembered some time afterwards that she had gone down to the lake after this prayer and had sat on a rock above a deep pool and for the first time had not even thought of leaping into the water.

It took some months for the physical symptoms of eczema and other difficulties to disappear. But she is now so completely healed as to be admitted to the mission field although the examining doctors were told her whole history. The verdict was, "I know of no one better fitted to be a missionary." She is so perfectly well and so filled with the Holy Spirit and with gifts of healing and of faith that she works side by side with her husband in a mental hospital. And I say: "Praise the Lord!"

Also I say to those of you troubled by uncomprehended fears and irrational thoughts and uncontrollable emotions: Satan cannot possess you if you have given your life to Jesus Christ and if you abstain from all witchcraft and spiritualism as the Bible commands you. One possesses you and one only: Jesus Christ the Son of God. Hold fast to Him and He will hold fast to you and will preserve you until such time as He can send to you one of those to whom He has given power over all manner of troubling spirits. Then through the prayer of such a faithful one, if there be any of the temptation of the Enemy left within you, He will conquer it completely and send it away.

And I say to you who long to heal the memories and to comfort the hearts of these who so need comfort—there is a power against which all the gates of hell shall not prevail and it is the power of the Holy Spirit of the Risen Christ. Walk with care until you are endued with power when the Holy Ghost comes upon you. Do you know Jesus? Does He know you? Is His Spirit your spirit? "Now if any man have not the Spirit of Christ, he is none of His." (Rom. 8:9.) If you are really filled with the Spirit of Jesus Christ then all lesser spirits will know you and will flee at your command and will loose any hold they have upon one whom they can never possess no matter how hard they try. And if by chance they are not evil but only lost ones, and if you send them forth not in anger but into the hands of Christ, then you know not what work you may be accomplishing in the unseen as well as in the seen. You, being in the flesh and adhering bravely to it, desiring not to see or to hear that which is forbidden, nevertheless may release into the hands of the Lord some lost and wandering soul who has held to the psyche of a living person in a vain attempt there to find life!

Once, in New Zealand, I prayed for a young woman who felt that her psyche was being torn apart with some infiltrating spirit. She had put herself in danger, if I recall correctly, by attending a séance. She stated that some familiar spirit had entered into her at that time and was pushing her personality almost to the wall. As she expressed it, "I have hardly room inside myself to be myself." This encroaching personality did not seem to be consciously evil. I spoke to it gently, therefore, advising it that this was not the place wherein it could find life and dismissing it with loving prayer into the hands of Christ.

The young woman said, "It spoke before it left. It said, 'I'm sorry! Good-bye!'"

One cannot prove of course that "it" really spoke. The woman's imagination may have dreamed up the words inside of her. But at any rate, she was healed.

12

Miracles

THE GIFT WHICH MOST OF ALL TESTIFIED TO THE HEATHEN world of the reality of the Holy Spirit was not the gift of tongues, but the gift of miracles. "He therefore that ministereth to you the Spirit, and worketh miracles among you . . ." (Gal. 3:5.) "And when they saw the mighty works that were done . . ." How often do phrases such as this run through the whole Bible! For, in the New Testament, God showed forth His Being and His power by moving not only upon the souls and the bodies of men but upon nature itself to do His will.

We have spoken of gifts of faith and gifts of healing—what, then, is the gift of miracles other than these?

The primary definition of "miracle" in Webster's unabridged dictionary is: "An event and effect in the physical world . . . deviating from the known laws of

nature or transcending our knowledge of these laws
. . . brought about by superhuman agency."

Many healings can hardly be called miracles, because they are completely understandable. Most doctors are cognizant of the intercommunication between
soul and body and the effect of each upon the other.
Most can see how, as the personality changes through
the prayer of faith and through Christian nurture, the
body grows into new life; the healing processes of the
body speeded up by a "superhuman" power that is yet
perfectly natural to us.

There are, however, healings that take place so
quickly and in ways that so completely transcend our
knowledge of the laws of nature that any honest
doctor would call them miracles. Or, if he deems that
word unethical, he might call them spontaneous remis-
sions.

For instance, there was a young woman in the
Framingham Union Hospital of Framingham, Massa-
chusetts. She had driven head on into a tree, after
skidding on ice, and the doctors pronounced her mori-
bund. She was bleeding from the eyes, ears, nose
and mouth; the lungs were filling; the pelvic bone was
broken in five places, crushed and driven up four
inches into her body, and she was cut internally
through the rectum and vagina. She was of course
unconscious, eyes rolled back, face slate-gray when I
went to see her and prayed with the laying on of
hands. She revived, but the next morning sank again,
and again I prayed for her. She was, moreover, surrounded by prayer: her sister who was her trained

nurse believed in God's healing power and so did her grandmother, mother, and aunt. One or more of these devoted women was continually with her while the men of the family lingered in the corridor waiting for her to die. The struggle for life went on for five days. At the end of five days, no medical or surgical treatment having been possible, the young woman was well. X rays showed no broken bones or inner lesions and all the processes of the body went on normally. Today, she walks with no limp whatever—and best of all, not only she but all the men of the family as well as the women have now returned to their church. They do not understand, but they know that God moved upon His world in a manner that could not be called other than miraculous.

Whether these miracles of healing "deviate from the known laws of nature" or whether they merely "transcend our knowledge of these laws," they are as amazing as the miracle of beauty in a snowflake, as thrilling as the miracle of jeweled living creatures in deep waters and of light that shines upon this earth from worlds that sent it forth a thousand years ago.

From time immemorial the Lord has done miracles through people. Through the obedience of Moses He rolled back the waters of the Red Sea. (Ex. 14:22.) Through the faith of Peter He sent an angel to unlock the prison doors. (Acts 12:4–11.) Through the word of Jesus Himself and of the servants who obeyed Him, He turned the water into wine. (John 2:1–11.) Through the faith of Jesus Christ again and of the disciples who continued breaking and passing out the bread, He increased the loaves and fishes until they fed five thousand people. (John 6:1–14.)

Through the faith of Jesus again He brought back life to the widow's son, to Jairus' daughter, and to Lazarus. One may wonder whether the little maid was in a coma or whether the widow's son was mistakenly diagnosed as dead. But there seems little doubt that Lazarus was most definitely dead. (John 11:39.) Jesus commanded His disciples to heal the sick and to *raise the dead.* Have any others besides Our Lord done this? Yes, even in the old days before He came bringing immortal life in His hands, Elisha, stormy prophet of Israel, brought life again to the son of the Shunammite woman, even breathing into his mouth as men do today in trying to bring back life to a drowned man. (II Kings 4:32–37.) And after the coming of the Holy Ghost, that greatest of healers, Saint Paul, whatever (or whoever) his own thorn in the flesh might have been, yet brought life and health to many, even to the young man who fell out of a window and broke his neck and died. (Acts 20:9–12.) And in modern days, a Negro woman minister of Philadelphia, and one of my friends, has twice in her ministry seen a resurrection. Also a resurrection took place through the service of baptism administered by my father-in-law. Summoned to baptize a dying child, he found the child already dead on his arrival. Whereupon he dropped the blessed water into the infant's mouth during baptism and prayed for life to return—and it did.

Even resurrection, then, is not unknown to the children of God. However, I can give you no rule concerning it nor can I hold forth any suggestion. I myself have never dared to pray for such a thing. But my heart lifts up when I know that even this is not beyond the scope of His powers.

But what about the other miracles I have mentioned: miracles affecting not man but the "lifeless" substance of wind and water, metal and food?

Who says it is lifeless?

The breath of God blows in the winds, the re-creating principle of life broods upon the waters, even metals radiate with an energy that cannot be seen, giving forth an infrared light. Even the life-principle that is in food can be blessed to our use, as we say with our lips every time we "say grace" or, more accurately, "ask the blessing."

When we are in God we are at one with these principles of life. To whatever extent we give ourselves to God He is able to give Himself through us to the world around us—and it is for this dominion that the very creature groans within itself waiting for the manifestation of the Sons of God. (Rom. 8:19.)

There is in the Air Force an officer of high rank among men and of even higher rank with God, for he has the gifts of the Holy Spirit and most particularly gifts of wisdom and knowledge and gifts of faith and of the working of miracles. He wondered, at one time, whether he should leave the service and go into the ministry. But God told him that He needed his ministry more in the Air Force than He did in a church—as God needs the ministry of many in factories and trucking businesses and department stores and schools.

Once, when flying in hurricane weather, he heard messages from someone high above the clouds and alone: "What can I do? I can't come down! I have no instruments! I can't see the ground! My gas is giving out! Someone tell me what to do!" It proved impossible to get a message through from the large Government plane to this little lost one. And of what use, after all, would a message have been? The officer spoke therefore to the winds and to the clouds. In prayer and in faith he directed them to move aside and let the plane through. Soon he heard another message, "Oh, there's a hole! I'm coming down!" He looked around. Three layers of clouds had rolled back like the waters of the Red Sea, and the little plane, like a mosquito, dived down toward the green earth below. Immediately the clouds rolled back again—like the water of the Red Sea.

The man in the little plane never dreamed that an officer of the Air Force in the name of the Lord had given orders to the clouds and the wind currents and that they had obeyed him!

Again, one day this officer continued in intensive prayer for he knew not what—while a student flyer crashed in flames, and walked out of the fire without a hurt or even the smell of fire upon his garments, precisely as did Shadrach, Meshach and Abednego. (Daniel 3:19–28.)

"But there must have been some natural law," you may be thinking. Very likely. God works through natural laws, bending them to His will and superimposing upon them laws that we as yet know not.

Perhaps you have known similar occurrences in automobile accidents or fires, and have wondered whether they were acts of God or merely coincidence.

When Jesus healed ten men of leprosy only one returned to give glory to God. I wonder whether the nine thought, "It must have been a strange coincidence?" And I wonder, if they did think thus, how much of the spiritual value of the healing they may have missed?

But come now, come now. Can I really possibly believe such crazy things—for instance that God sent a heavenly messenger and unlocked the prison doors while the prayer group prayed for Peter's deliverance? Can God's power really affect *things?* Clouds and fire and even material substances such as metal? Well, yes. (Many of you know that it can, but are afraid to say so lest people think you queerer than you really are.) It is possible even for the molecular structure of objects that appear to us quite unyielding to be changed by the power of God.

For instance, I know a young veterinarian who arrived at a dinner party in his Chevrolet while his wife drove from another direction in their Chrysler. On leaving the car he managed somehow to leave the key within it and to shut the doors so that they automatically locked. When a hurry call came from the hospital that one of his patients (who happened to be a dog) needed quick care, he could not open the door of his car. Doubtless he prayed for the dog whose tourniquet had slipped out of place. And while he was in prayer and still struggling with the car door, a voice said within him, "Take the Chrysler key and open the Chevrolet." He took the Chrysler key and opened the door of the Chevrolet. But never again would the key to his wife's car open his own car.

Now you are perfectly at liberty to reject this simple story of God's grace if you care to do so. And this is not the kind of miracle concerning which I can say, "Try it and see." For we are strictly forbidden to test God by asking for a useless sign. Even Jesus Himself would not cast Himself from the temple roof when tempted by Satan. But I can only say: when we need such a miracle, it can happen. A friend was once driving to the station to meet my train when she felt and heard a slow leak in a tire. "O Lord, if you'll just hold it till I get to the station," she prayed, "I promise I'll go to the garage right away and get it fixed."

"Lady," said the puzzled attendant, after a careful scrutiny of the wheel, "there's nothing the matter with your tire!"

My friend had asked only for a bit of protection, not for a repair job upon the tire. But apparently the power of the Lord in protecting the tire had so altered the vibrating energy of which its matter was made that it needed no further repair.

It would be hard on garagemen everywhere if the laws that govern such action were known, would it not?

Peter walked upon the water once, when Jesus gave him permission to do so, but never again. Of course I believe that he walked upon the water! He no doubt was upheld by the same principle of levitation (lightening the weight of the body) that Jesus Himself knew how to use. Instances of this have happened throughout the lives of the saints. "Put me down, Lord!" Saint Theresa is reported to have cried before the altar as the little nuns ran to catch her skirts. "Enough of this nonsense!" But as a known principle of getting from here to there, it cannot be used. We are far too earthbound. Besides, think of the loss to airplane companies.

What is the use, then, of writing about the gift of miracles if I cannot say, "Pray this way and that, and such and such a miracle will happen?" Firstly, that we may believe. For our belief will hold a door open within us so that in God's good time and in God's good will He can move through us even to alter the course of nature. Secondly—and perhaps it is the same thing—so that we can be deeply comforted, knowing that God is not without resources even when we can see none of them. God can make a way where there isn't a way. If we have reached the uppermost limit of our powers He can send the right person to help us even from the ends of the earth and even if that person has to cut down trees to earn the money for the trip. If the forces of this world—wind and water, fire and snow—are reaching out to us in order to destroy us, He can move upon those forces and they will move.

My sister-in-law once stood with hose in hand spraying the roof of her Hollywood home to protect it from sparks of fire.

A lone car whizzed up the canyon road and stopped momentarily.

"Lady, *get away!*" cried a man, leaning from the window. "You'll be burned to a crisp!"

"No, I won't!" she yelled back and stood her ground.

The next minute the wind changed and, instead of blowing the fire straight up the canyon to the destruction of many homes besides hers, blew the fire away across the hills where the firefighters could conquer it.

But what of the other miracles that Jesus did: the changing the water into wine, for instance? Are we really to believe that He performed such an utterly unnecessary work as this? Surely if they lacked wine and He grieved for their embarrassment He might have found a more practical way of helping them! If we had been there we could have said, "Well now, I'd like to give a little present to the bride" and fished in our pockets for some bills. . . .

Can we believe that a spiritual power can actually enter into *water* and change it in quality?

What do we mean when we say or hear the priest say at a baptism, "Sanctify this water to the mystical washing away of sin"? Surely we should believe what we say: that a spiritual power actually enters into the water and imparts to it a re-creating power far more mysterious than the natural power of wine. And possibly Our Lord, in addition to taking pity on the host's embarrassment, meant also to show us a spiritual power for the washing away even of the inherited sins and weaknesses of the race, that new life may enter the soul and the body of the one baptized.

What, again, of the multiplying of food? Have I ever known cases of the actual expansion of matter? Yes, I have. There is the well-authenticated case of Corrie Ten Boom, a prisoner of war and a woman great in prayer and in forgiveness, who kept many prisoners alive with one bottle of vitamins which never decreased—so that she doled out the golden drops day by day, and, as the next day came, she could dole them out again. . . .

"There must be some physical explanation. . . ." Possibly. Try and find it.

But there is no physical explanation of the words we hear when we receive the bread that He has blessed at the altar: "May this . . . preserve thy soul and body unto everlasting life." Has that bread received a preserving—a life-giving and life-extending quality— which, if we believe it, can preserve and extend life in us?

This is what we hear with our ears. Can we believe it with our hearts? Maybe such is the truth that He meant to show us on that day long ago, atop a hill, when the disciples, never faltering, broke the bread and passed it to row after row of people, believing always that it would continue to increase.

It is not given to us, except possibly in dire emergency, to bless actual bread so that it will increase. We are not as yet to be trusted with so much power. We would be sure to use it greedily and in disobedience even as certain of the Israelites did in the wilderness when the food bred worms and stank. But if we dare to believe, if we dare to believe. . . . If we could grasp the idea that God is in His universe and that the blood of the Lamb covers the earth, redeeming even nature and restoring it to that perfect obedience to the will of God in which it was created, then we ourselves would be His new creation, the crowning glory of His universe.